The Authorities
Powerful Wisdom from Leaders in the Field

HERMAN SIU & MARTIN SIU

©2014 by 10-10-10 Publishing

All rights reserved. No part of this publication may be reproduced or transmitted in any form or by any means, electronic or mechanical, including photocopying, recording, or any other information storage and retrieval system without the written permission of the publisher and author.

Published by
10-10-10 Publishing
1-9225 Leslie St.
Richmondhill, ON
L4B 3H6
Canada

Printed in the United States of America.
ISBN: 1927677955

FOREWORD

Experts are to be admired for their knowledge, but they often remain unrecognized by the general public because they save their information and insights for paying customers and clients. There are many experts in a given field, but their impact is limited to the handful of people with whom they work.

Unlike experts, authorities share their knowledge and expertise far more broadly, so they make a big impact on the world. Authorities become known and admired as leading experts and, as such, typically do very well economically and professionally. Most authorities are also mature enough to know that part of the joy of monetary success is the accompanying moral and spiritual obligation to give back.

Many people want to learn and work with well-respected and generous authorities, but don't always know where to find them. They may be known to their peers, or within a specific community, but have not had the opportunity to reach a wider audience. At one time, they might have submitted a proposal to the For Dummies or Chicken Soup for the Soul series of books, but it's now almost impossible to get accepted as a new author in such branded book series.

It is more than fitting that Raymond Aaron, an internationally known and respected authority in his own right, would be the one to recognize the need for a new venue in which authorities could share their considerable knowledge with readers everywhere. As the only author ever to be included in both of the book series mentioned above, Raymond has had the opportunity to give back and he understands how crucial it is for authorities to have a platform from which to share their expertise.

I have known and worked with Raymond for a number of years and consider him a valued friend and talented coach. He knows how to spot talented and knowledgeable people and he desires to see them prosper. Over the years, success coaching and speaking engagements around the world have made it possible for Raymond to meet many of these talented authorities. He recognizes and relates to their passion and enthusiasm for what they do, as well as their desire to share what they know. He tells me that's why he created this new nonfiction branded book series, The Authorities.

Dr. Nido Qubein
President, High Point University

TABLE OF CONTENTS

Introduction V

The Modern Healer 1
Herman Siu and Martin Siu

Branding Small Business 19
Raymond Aaron

Happiness: How to Experience the "Real Deal"s 33
Marci Shimoff

Sex, Love and Relationships 43
Dr. John Gray

A Dream Life for the Asking 49
Tom Barber

Downsize Into a Better, More Fulfilling Rest of Your Life 59
Monika Lowry & Robert Miller

Have More Money, More Clients and More Freedom
by Going Digital 69
Ashar Alam

Create the Life of Your Dreams 77
Dexter Montgomery & Pamela Montgomery

Keep Your Job & Get Promoted …Guaranteed. 87
Frantz Forestal

Evolution of Consciousness for the Entrepreneur 95
Audree Tara Weitzman

Declutter Your Mind For Success 107
Erin Muldoon Stetson

The Print Management Specialist 121
Thomas J. Samuelson

INTRODUCTION

This book introduces you to *The Authorities* — individuals who have distinguished themselves in life and in business. Authorities make a big impact on the world. Authorities are leaders in their chosen fields. Authorities typically do very well financially, and are evolved enough to know that part of the joy of monetary success is the accompanying social, moral and spiritual obligation to give back.

Authorities are not just outstanding. They are also *known* to be outstanding.

This additional element begins to explain the difference between two strategic business and life concepts — one that seems great, but isn't, and the other that fills in the essential missing gap of the first.

The first concept is "the expert."

What is an expert? The real definition is ...

EXPERT: *a person who knows stuff*

People who have attained a very senior academic degree (like a PhD or an MD) definitely know stuff. People who read voraciously and retain what they read definitely know stuff. Unfortunately, just because you know stuff does not mean that anyone respects the fact that you do. Even though some experts are successful, alas, most are not — because knowing stuff is not enough.

Well, then, what is the missing piece?

What the expert lacks, "the authority" has. The authority both knows stuff and is *known* to know stuff. So, more simply ...

AUTHORITY: *a person who is known as an expert*

The difference is not subtle. The difference is not merely semantic. The difference is enormous.

When it comes to this subject, there are actually three categories in which people fall:

- People who don't know much and are unsuccessful in life and in business. Most people fall in this category.

- People who know stuff, but still don't leave much of a footprint in the world. There are a lot of people like this.

- Experts who are also *known* as experts become authorities and authorities are always wondrously successful. Authorities are able to contribute more to humanity through both their chosen work and their giving back.

This book is about the highest category, *The Authorities* — people who have reached the peak in their field and are known as such.

You will definitely know some of *The Authorities* in this book, especially since there are some world-famous ones. Others are just as exceptional, but you may not yet know about them. Our featured authors, for example, are Dr. Martin Siu and Herman Siu, a father-son team who incorporate old-world healing practices inherited through generations of family healers. They help their patients become Modern Healers, by empowering them to take back control of and responsibility for their health with healing and wellness modalities that represent the cumulative wisdom of centuries of medical ancestors. If you would like to learn more about Martin and Herman, visit http://omaniclinic.com.

Read each chapter carefully to learn and to see the business potential that may be possible between yourself and each one of *The Authorities*. You may well be able to become their client or, possibly, do business with them in other ways.

They are *The Authorities*. Learn from them. Connect with them. Let them uplift you. Learning from them and working with them is the secret ingredient for success which may well allow you too to rise to the level of Authority soon.

To be considered for inclusion in a subsequent edition of *The Authorities*, register to attend a 2-Day Wealth Tycoon Workshop at www.TwoDayTycoon.com, where you will be interviewed and considered.

The Modern Healer

Herman Siu & Martin Siu

Good health is a God-given right; it's our birthright. Yet, while we have made huge technological advances to facilitate cross-planet communication in real-time, we haven't been as progressive in keeping ourselves healthy.

We may be living longer but, tragically, children are dying from cancers, diabetes is on the rise, and young adults are suddenly getting heart attacks. Chronic fatigue, depression, and anxiety assail us. We rely on drugs to fix our health problems and we spend billions of dollars on prescriptions that may alleviate the symptoms but leave the root cause untouched. In our fast-paced societies, we have lost the connection with nature and the natural elements that make up our bodies. Surely, there is an alternative way to heal ourselves, or even to prevent disease from occurring in the first place.

The long and short of it is that we don't have to drop out of society and reside in the woods to live happier and healthier lives. The answer to good health and longevity lies right at our fingertips – in the air we breathe, the foods we eat, and water we drink. That's the best prescription for the Modern Healer, and these are the guiding principles we use in our healing practice. As 5th and 6th generation healers immersed in traditions that date back to ancient Chinese Shaolin practices, we adhere to the disciplined and holistic approach of our forefathers.

We believe that a body in full balance has everything it needs to fight off disease, stay and look young, and be active and involved, regardless of the biological age. This belief has been supported by patient outcomes through successive centuries of practice by the healers in our family. We share this knowledge with you to empower you as a Modern Healer, so that you may take control of and assume responsibility for your own health and be the expert in your own healing and wellness journey.

To be empowered as a Modern Healer, you must first understand the core concepts of energy or Qi (chi) as defined by ancient Chinese healing texts.

Dr. Paul Unschuld, a highly-regarded authority on Chinese medicine and multi-book author said, "The core Chinese concept of qi bears no resemblance to the Western concept of 'energy'. We perceive that there is a knowledge gap in the current understanding of eastern medicine in the western world. Mindful of the wisdom suggested by the Chinese proverb, "A journey of a thousand miles begins with a single step," we have written this chapter as our first step towards bridging that divide.

There are three primary components to balance Qi. Qi is a fundamental power underlying all of nature, and it is a vital life force that runs through our body. There are three primary components to balance our Qi. The first component to boosting our Qi is the air we breathe, the second is the food we eat, and the third is the water we drink.

AIR GIVES LIFE

Almost all of life needs oxygen to survive. We take in oxygen from our surroundings to harness energy and use it to power the inner workings of our bodies.

In the Huangdi Neijing, the ancient Chinese foundation medical text, the lungs breathe in what's known as, da qi, or "great qi.". Once we breathe in the air, the lungs extract the Qi from the da qi. Based on this understanding, we perceive that Qi relates to life-sustaining oxygen.

What is the secret to having great Qi? It is the harmonization of the mind, body, and spirit.

In martial arts, we use our mind to harness Qi by controlling our breath. We use our body to breathe, and we put our bodies through constant practice to master our Qi. Once it has been mastered, the Qi can be at our fingertips in a moment's notice. We call it in this form the spirit.

Viewed from this perspective, it's simple to make the most of living and get the best use of your life. The first step to taking back control of your health is by learning to breathe correctly.

Notice, right this moment, how you are breathing. Are you breathing from your diaphragm or the stomach, or are you taking in quick snatches of air? The majority of us take shallow breaths because we have forgotten how to breathe deeply and fully, and the only time we do so is when we are in yoga or meditation. Having become a society of superficial breathers, we are not benefitting from the fact that 70% of the toxins in our bodies are released through breath. By breathing shallowly, we are shortchanging ourselves because hypoxia, or insufficient oxygen in the body's cells, has been linked to degenerative diseases.

Remember, breath equals life and a long breath enhances a long life. Breathing correctly is your first responsibility as a Modern Healer.

FOOD FOR HEALING

The second primary component to balance our Qi is food.

The ancient Greek physician, Hippocrates, who is widely known as the "Father of Medicine", is quoted as saying "Let food be thy medicine and medicine be thy food." Fast forward several centuries; Dr. Roger J. Williams, who discovered the B-vitamin, said in 1971, "The human body heals itself and nutrition provides the resources to accomplish the task." The Chinese are well known to eat their food in its season. For example, no watermelon is eaten in winter since it grows in the hot summer climate.

It is empowering to discover that we need look no further than our own gardens and our kitchens to find healing nutrition that supports health for our family. By making healthy food choices, we ensure that we age gracefully and live out the rest of the twilight years harmoniously and peacefully, without the blight of Alzheimer's, dementia, or other failing diseases.

> *"So many people spend their health gaining wealth & then have to spend their wealth to regain their health."* - Chinese proverb

Our philosophy is that, with right air, right food and right water (in this order), you detoxify naturally, without having to go on rigid short-term fasts.

With the right balance of foods that are appropriate to your body type, you'll get rid of excess fat and flab, find the correct body weight, be brimming over with energy, have the mental clarity to solve challenges with ease, and be in love with your life.

If you're tired of feeling frustrated, angry, depressed, unsure, overweight, tired, and in despair, look to your shopping list, refrigerator and kitchen closets for the culprits. Are they full of processed foods and refined sugars? Are you eating natural grains, green leafy vegetables and fresh fruit?

In this chapter, we'll draw on healing secrets that we share with our clients in our Toronto-based clinic. We'll discuss the major foods that prevent inflammation, help you recover from cuts and wounds, and help detoxify the system.

But for the Modern Healer, the first line of defense is maintaining a healthy pH balance. Acid is corrosive and is the biggest culprit of many degenerative and deadly diseases. It's true that some acid is needed in the body. The stomach uses it to break down the food we eat into macronutrients such as proteins, fats and carbohydrates, and micronutrients such as vitamins and minerals that it may be easily absorbed by the body. But most typical diets are packed with sugar, animal proteins, and processed foods.

WHY PH BALANCE IS CRUCIAL TO GOOD HEALTH

The pH is a measure of acidity or alkalinity. The billions of cells that make up our bodies need an alkaline environment to function, to stay healthy, and to regenerate. Too much acid in our bodies creates ripe conditions for the growth of bacteria, yeast, fungus, viruses, mold and other diseases. Cells that are starved of oxygen are unable to regenerate. Once starved, they are unable to repair damage or rid the body of noxious chemicals and toxins. In time, the cells die; research now points out that cancer is the result of an over-acidic body. An ideal balance for our bodies is measured between a pH of 7.2 – 7.4. You can measure this by dipping pH testing strips into a sample of saliva or urine. An acidic body will produce a pH reading of less than 7.2, which means there is a lack of oxygenation at the cellular level. Your body may even create more fat cells to store the corrosive acid, leading to unwanted weight gain. If the body is malnourished or lacking any Alkaline minerals, it goes in search of calcium to optimize the pH level, and extracts calcium from your bones (joints), teeth and tissues which in turn leaves the bones weak. Calcium is one of the most important alkaline minerals as it increases the oxygen level in the blood. This calcium depletion results in arthritis and osteoporosis. In the initial stages of over-acidity, you may suffer from joint pains, headaches, and weight gain. In an acidic state, the body is trying to expel excess acid through your skin, causing muscle cramps, eczema, acne, swelling, irritation, and general aches and pains. People in this state get grouchier and irritable, and they age faster than those with a balanced pH body. Other so-called modern diseases linked to an acidic body include diabetes, osteoarthritis, acid reflux, irritable bowel syndrome, premature aging, muscle and chronic fatigue, bone loss and osteoporosis.

"The only way to keep good health is to eat what you don't want, drink what you don't like, & do what you'd rather not" -Chinese proverb

GETTING YOUR PH BALANCE RIGHT THROUGH FOODS

Our experience has shown that a balanced diet should be 85-90% alkaline and 10-15% acidic. Body functions and hand-eye coordination work at their optimal state at these levels. It's better for the body to be slightly alkaline than it is to be slightly acidic. Now that we understand why the pH balance is the first line of defense and why it's crucial to maintain the correct pH balance, let's explore quickly what foods contribute to a more alkaline state and more acidic state. A food is classified as alkaline or acidic according to its mineral content. Alkaline-forming foods contain more minerals such as calcium, magnesium, manganese, iron, and potassium. Some acid-promoting minerals include phosphorous, copper, and sulfur. Carbonated drinks are acid forming because they are loaded with sugar and phosphorus, which can lead to weight gain. Have a healthy serving of kale or broccoli instead, which nourishes your body with helpful calcium and magnesium for bone and muscle health. Alkaline foods include apples, apricots, cantaloupes, cauliflower, broccoli, kale, almonds, chestnuts and walnuts. The complete list is much longer and we will examine the healing qualities of alkaline-based nutrition in the section under Anti-Inflammation Foods. Acidic foods include ice-cream, manufactured processed foods with refined sugar, meat, fish, poultry, and eggs. This is not to say that all fruits and vegetables are alkaline. Some are in fact very acidic. Acidic vegetables include corn, onions, and garlic. In the fruit category will fall cranberries, blueberries, and currants. As you grow older, it's harder to expel the acid that is in your body. The longer acid exists, the more it will congeal and the more it will attack your cells and immune system. Acidic conditions manifest one illness at a time. Symptoms include arthritis, muscle fatigue, and body aches. At the point that you are weakest is when you're most prone to infections and diseases because infections live off acidic waste products. At our clinic, we will examine the root cause of your health problems, not just the symptoms. We will customize a holistic healing plan drawing on our experience and expertise to restore you to the right balance, homeostasis, so you may live your life in joy and harmony.

"Tell me and I'll forget; show me and I may remember; involve me and I'll understand" - Chinese proverb

ALKALINE AND ANTI-INFLAMMATION FOODS

Inflammation is a natural body response to injury. You bruise when you hit your shin against a table leg or when you sprain an ankle. Chronic inflammation, if undetected, can result in debilitating illnesses such as heart disease, cancer, diabetes, arthritis, and Alzheimer's. Fried and processed foods, as well as foods that contain trans-fat, increase the risk of inflammation. We've mentioned that alkaline foods prevent inflammation, and these are ordinary fruits, vegetables, and herbs that you can find in your refrigerator, spice cabinet, and even in your own garden. There are many creative ways to prepare these foods for a delicious, nutritious, beneficial anti-inflammation diet/alkaline diet. Here is a small list of foods to keep your body in balance and in good health.

Avocados: they contain healthy fats, phyto-proteins, vitamins, minerals and dietary fiber that is sorely lacking in the western societies. Low in sugar content, avocados may help to lower cholesterol levels, and increase resistance to diabetes, coronary heart disease, stroke and cancer, while promoting a healthy body weight and body mass index (BMI). Avocados are best eaten fresh.

Bamboo shoots: which is not a common vegetable on the western table, were identified by the Compendium of Materia Medica, the most comprehensive medical book in the history of traditional Chinese Medicine. Bamboo shoots promote the circulatory system, supplementing the body's natural energy, and are recommended as a daily dish. A traditional forest vegetable in Chinese diets for 2,500 years, nutrient-rich bamboo shoots are being shown in modern research to help prevent cancer, and to aid in weight loss, digestion, and the appetite.

Bamboo shoots are rich in essential amino acids and fatty acids and, because of their low sugar content, they are useful for treating hypertension, hyperlipemia, and hyperglycemia.

Broccoli: just about all vegetables are good, but some are more alkaline than others. Broccoli counts among the latter as it is rich in important vitamins such as A, C, K, B-complex and minerals including iron, zinc, and phosphorus. Broccoli is also rich in phytonutrients, which are natural chemicals that help protect plants and prevent disease in our bodies.

Broccoli helps to prevent osteoarthritis, reduces the risk of cancer, and has been shown to help reverse diabetes and heart damage. Broccoli is best lightly steamed or gently stir-fried; overcooking will neutralize its benefits.

Cabbage: A source of Vitamins K, C, B6, folate, and thiamine. Cabbage is also a source of iodine to support the health of the brain and the nervous system. This vegetable, which is a staple in Chinese kitchens around the world, helps to lower cholesterol and is rich in glucosinolates that are shown to have cancer prevention properties.

Carrot: Raw or cooked, carrots are a rich source of Vitamins A and C, calcium and iron, and the anti-oxidant beta-carotene that gives the vegetable its orange colour. In addition, carrots contain fibre, Vitamins K and E, potassium, folate, manganese, magnesium, zinc, and some phosphorus. Carrots improve our vision, delay aging, help with regulating blood sugar, improve digestion, and help prevent cancer. There is a side note to add: overconsumption of carrots can be toxic so, if you start turning orange, you may want to cut back on your carrot intake!

Cauliflower: The cauliflower is packed with vitamins such as B1, B2, B3,

B5, B6, B9, C and K, as well as being rich in omega 3, fatty acids, fibre, manganese, and potassium. Apart from delivering powerful antioxidants, cauliflower is a healthy source of protein and fibre, it enhances the body's ability to detoxify, reduces the risk of inflammation and the incidence of cancer. Cauliflower is best lightly cooked through a simple sauté.

Spinach: Spinach is widely acknowledged to be rich in vitamins and minerals such as magnesium, iron, copper, calcium, potassium, and zinc. The dark green spinach is packed with anti-oxidants and health-promoting phytonutrients. If you're low in iron, spinach helps to make up the deficit. It is an aid in the management of diabetes, and works towards lowering high blood pressure and improving bone health. Spinach is best eaten lightly steamed, quickly boiled or sautéed.

Ginger: Mankind's historic cure-all, ginger is rich in anti-oxidants, vitamins and minerals, and also contains omega-3 and omega-6. Shown to be anti-inflammatory, anti-cancer, anti-nausea, and a powerful anti-oxidant, it greatly boosts the immune system. A versatile root, ginger can be chewed fresh, steamed, boiled in water to make tea, or grated and added to sautéed dishes.

The state in which it is consumed will affect its benefits greatly. Fresh ginger root fights the common cold, coughs, and asthma, while dried ginger root is better against abdominal pain, cold limbs, and rheumatism. If you were to use the fresh root for rheumatism, the condition will worsen but, fresh or dried, it is effective in preventing or stopping vomiting and diarrhea. Large quantities of fresh ginger are not recommended for those with high blood pressure, inflammatory bowel disease, ulcers, or intestinal blockage, and should be used sparingly if you suffer from gallstones. Excessive consumption can cause a person to break out in a rash as an allergic reaction and may also lead to heartburn, bloating, gas, belching, and even some nausea. From ginger root, we'll move on to alkaline-forming fruit and herbs to round up our short list of recommended foods. Remember, some foods are mildly acidic and some are weak acidic foods. Not all acidic foods are tarred with the same brush, but the worst offenders include processed foods, sugar, tomatoes, onions, garlic, dairy, and vinegar.

Apricot: the fruit and the seeds are effective alkaline-forming foods. Packed with iron and protein, apricots are good for quenching thirst and fighting asthma. The seeds from the bitter apricot heal coughs, sore throats, and constipation, as does the sweet apricot seed. But those suffering from asthma should eat only the bitter apricot seed, or the condition will worsen. Laetrile, a naturally occurring substance found in the kernels, has been increasingly promoted to help in cancer treatment. The apricot kernels have been documented to help fight against tumors as far back as 502 AD. The apricot oil has been used as far back as 17th century England to fight swellings, tumors, and ulcers

Peppermint: a herb with healing benefits dating back to ten thousand years in the past, peppermint is commonly used to fight inflammation. It soothes abdominal pain, indigestion, irritable bowels and bloating, and prevents nausea and vomiting. It is a popular healing food for the common colds that are accompanied by headaches, sore throat and thick phlegm. However, if you are suffering a common cold but have a runny nose, cold limbs and diarrhea, peppermint is not that effective. Although it is commonly thought of as an herb or a spice, it is actually cool and pungent, and should not be used daily. Those suffering from anemia or low blood pressure should use only as directed.

"Health is the greatest gift, Contentment is the greatest treasure, Confidence is the greatest friend, Enlightenment is the greatest bliss." -Chinese proverb

FOODS TO ACCELERATE HEALING OF CUTS AND WOUNDS

Skin is the biggest organ in our bodies, and we tend to take it for granted because small nicks heal quickly. However, there are times when there is a deep cut or wound from an accident or from surgery when extra support is required for the connective tissue to regenerate. Connective tissue is different from most other tissues because it is made not so much of cells, but from protein, notably collagen, fibres encased in a unique covering called a fascia. To boost your ability to heal quickly from cuts and wounds, look for foods with these four pivotal nutrients and minerals.

Vitamin C: Vitamin C assists in forming collagen to repair the connective tissue in the blood vessels, cartilage, muscles, and in the bones. Good sources of Vitamin C include fruits such as guava, kiwi, strawberries, and papaya. Vegetables include red and green sweet peppers, Brussels sprouts, broccoli, cauliflower, and sweet potatoes.

Vitamin A: Some of the foods mentioned in the category above will be useful for sourcing Vitamin A because they are rich beta-carotene that is converted into fully active Vitamin A. This vitamin serves many functions. It promotes growth, maintains the immune system, and supports vision. Other Vitamin A rich foods are sweet potatoes, pumpkins, carrots, spinach, turnip greens, and cantaloupe.

Flavonoids: These are a group of pigments that give plants their colour but are compounds that have been discovered to have anti-oxidant properties that are more powerful against a wider range of oxidants than the traditional antioxidants. They help the body detoxify, reduce inflammation, and prevent and reduce damage at the cellular level. Within this grouping, it's the flavonoid called catechin, which is found in great abundance in tea leaves, that is thought to inhibit the growth of cancerous cells. In addition to green, black, and oolong teas, flavonoids are also found in dark coloured berries, bananas, all citrus fruits, parsley, gingko biloba, and cocoa with chocolate content exceeding 70%.

Zinc: This mineral repairs damaged tissues and aids in healing wounds by generating proteins and other genetic material, boosts cell division andcollagen formation, and regenerates tissue, all of which are crucial to wound repair. It boosts the system, develops and activates the T-cells that fight off infection. Zinc is found in vegetables, nuts and seeds such as asparagus, bamboo shoots, Brussels sprouts, okra, potatoes, pumpkin, Swiss chard, lima beans, peas, pine nuts, cashews, pumpkin, and sunflower seeds.

KEEPING YOUR BRAIN HEALTHY

Fernando Gómez-Pinilla, professor of neurosurgery and physiological science in UCLA, describes food as a "pharmaceutical compound that affects the brain".

Studies conducted by him show that the brain is highly susceptible to oxidation damage, so foods that are high in antioxidants protect the brain cells from damage and dysfunction.

Omega-3 fatty acids: These fatty acids support the plasticity of the synapses in the brain that affect critical functions. These include learning and memory, fighting off depression, bipolar disorders, schizophrenia, and attention-deficit disorders. The particularly important omega-3 fatty acid is docosahexaenoic acid or DHA, which reduces oxidative damage, improves synapse plasticity, and is needed in the brain's cell membranes. Omega-3s are found abundantly in walnuts, avocados, flaxseed, chia, and kiwi fruit. Though typically recommended as a desirable source of fatty acids, we take a strong stand against salmon as a source of omega-3s. The oceans are filled with toxins such as mercury, dioxin, and more recently radiation, and seafood is filled with these dangerous elements. In our annals of healing, this leads to mental and neurological disorders such as dementia, Alzheimer's, and multiple sclerosis. It is much safer and healthier to find the fatty acids in nuts and fruit.

Folic Acid: The brain needs sufficient folic acid for its functions, and folate deficiency leads to depression and cognitive impairment. Combining folic acid with other B vitamins has been effective in slowing the rate of age-related decline in cognitive function, and in preventing dementia. Folic acid is found in green leafy vegetables such as spinach, asparagus, romaine, dried or fresh beans and peas, as well as in avocados, beets, broccoli, peanuts, sunflower seeds, honeydew melons, cantaloupes, bananas, raspberries, and grapefruits.

FOODS FOR DETOXIFICATION

In our view, a good detoxification is much more than a spring-cleaning. It's like a good oil change – you take out the gunk and replace it with good, clean nutrients that power the body.

We design tailored and customized detoxification programs that both cleanse and support your system. The concept behind our programs is that it's not enough just to flush out the toxins with a juice cleanse. Instead, you need to simultaneously put back nourishment and support that will revitalize and energize the organs and the immune system.

With that being said, the key organ that is most prone to work overload is the liver. The liver supports almost every organ in the body. It is the second largest organ in the body, and any alcohol or drugs taxes it severely. When that happens, the liver performs less than optimally, leading to an accumulation of toxins that in turn cause chronic illnesses. Natural detoxification foods and herbs are best prescribed after a complete diagnosis to know what is best for your body constitution.

Natural diuretics: Foods that flush the body of toxins are essential to a good detoxification or to counteract the effects of an unhealthy lifestyle. Among natural diuretics are watercress, dandelions in the form of tea, celery, and cabbage, in which is found the antioxidant glutathione to improve the liver's detoxifying function. Be advised that natural diuretics must be used with care; the amount and type to be consumed will depend on your individual body type and constitution.

THE TRUTH ABOUT WATER

The third component to balance our Qi is water.

Water covers 71% of the Earth's surface and is vital to all forms of life. Your body ranges between 50-75% of water as body composition varies according to gender and fitness level, because adipose tissue contains less water than lean tissue. Suffering from fuzzy short-term recall, having problems with mental math or reading small print? Those are signs of dehydration. Be careful in your choice of what you drink. Tap water, sodas, and coffee are all acidic. Our rule is 8x8. We recommend drinking at least eight 8-oz. glasses of water a day to neutralize the acid in the bloodstream for better metabolism and more efficient absorption of nutrients. For those looking for alkaline water, we prefer AquaHydrate, which has a pH of 9+, but only use as directed.

"When you are sick of sickness, you are no longer sick." -Chinese proverb

BE AN EMPOWERED MODERN HEALER

We hope this journey into the healing properties of good nutrition will empower you to make the right choices. Whether it is to give you more energy, get you thinking clearly, accelerate recovery from illnesses, or to age with grace, the choice to eat well and live well rests in your hands. You may find the way ahead difficult and you may need a boost to get you started on the right footing. You may have inexplicable aches, pains, or chronic colds and allergies that just simply refuse to go away. Just changing your diet is not enough to get you on the healing path. Whether you seek preventative care or deep healing, we have the alternative modalities to help you with the healing transformation.

The body is a finely-tuned mechanism. It works until it is out of balance and, even then, it seeks to right itself until the imbalance has buried itself too deeply. Once it does, we are assailed with all forms of diseases and ailments, some too deep to be cured with just nutrition.

As practitioners, we tap into the secrets of our forefathers, into healing practices that have been refined and polished and provided to thousands and thousands of patients through six generations of healers. These are intricate and sophisticated methods of diagnosis, healing, and remedies that are the result of centuries of observation and practice that have withstood the tests of time and the tests of western medicine.

We are deeply immersed in a culture of healing and we drill down to the causes of disease and illness by identifying patterns of disharmony in your body. Our methods are gentle and non-invasive, and we examine not just the visible symptoms, but also take into account the subtle, intangible forces that make up all life. As healers deeply ingrained in a compassionate practice, we examine the physical, mental, emotional, and spiritual aspects because the body, mind, and spirit are inseparable. When you consult with us, you benefit not just from our knowledge and experience, but also from the cumulative wisdom and healing of our medical ancestors.

Martin and Herman are 5th and 6th generation healers steeped in Chinese healing traditions preserved through a lineage that dates back to Shaolin Buddhist principles. As father and son, they run their Toronto-based clinic on a mission to bridge the ancient and modern worlds to take healing to the next level. They seek to bring the body's energies to balance through a holistic and compassionate approach to healing. They customize nutritional plans and draw on modalities such as acupuncture and Tong Ren, a specialized energy therapy, Qi Gong breathing and exercise routines to empower the patient in the healing journey. They are currently co-authoring an upcoming book in response to overwhelming demand from their clients. It will be a thorough look at the beneficial properties, compounds, antioxidants, and micronutrients found in food, and will include ancient breathing and exercise secrets that assist in the healing process. Get more information at http://omaniclinic.com.

Branding Small Business

RAYMOND AARON

Branding is an incredibly important tool for creating and building your business. Large companies have been benefiting from branding ever since people first started selling things to other people. Branding made those businesses big.

If you're a small business owner, you probably imagine that small companies are different and don't need branding as much as large companies do. Not true. The truth is small businesses need branding just as much, if not more, than large companies.

Perhaps you've thought about branding, but assumed you'd need millions of dollars to do it properly, or that branding is just the same thing as marketing. Nothing could be further from the truth.

Marketing is the engine of your company's success. Branding is the fuel in that engine.

In the old days, salespeople were a big part of the selling process. They recommended one product over another and laid out the reasons why it was better. Salespeople had credibility because they knew about all the products, and customers often took the advice they had to offer.

Today, consumers control the buying process. They shop in big box stores, super-sized supermarkets, and over the Internet — where there are no salespeople. Buyers now get online and gather information beforehand. They learn about all the products available and look to see if there really is any difference between them. Consumers also read reviews and check social media to see if both the company and the product are reputable. In other words, they want to know what the brand is all about.

The way of commerce used to be: "Nothing happens till something is sold." Today it's: "Nothing happens till something is branded!"

DEFINING A BRAND

A brand is a proper name that stands for something. It lives in the consumer's mind, has positive or negative characteristics, and invokes a feeling or an image. In short, it's a person's perception of a product or a company.

When all goes well, consumers associate the same characteristics with a brand that the company talks about in its advertising, public relations, marketing and sales materials. Of course, when a product doesn't live up to what the company says about it, the brand gets a bad reputation. On the other hand, if a product or service over-delivers on the promises made, the brand can become a superstar.

RECOGNIZING BRANDING AND ITS CHARACTERISTICS

Branding is the science and art of making something that isn't unique, unique. Branding in the marketplace is the same as branding on a ranch. On a ranch, ranchers use branding to differentiate their cattle from every other rancher's cattle (because all cattle look pretty much the same). In the marketplace, branding is what makes a product stand out in a crowd of similar products. The right branding gets you noticed, remembered and sold — or perhaps I should say bought, because today it is all about buying, not selling.

There are four main characteristics of branding that make it an integral part of the marketing and purchasing process.

1. Branding makes you trustworthy and known

Branding makes a product more special than other products. With branding, a normal, everyday product has a personality, and a first and last name, and people know who you are.

In today's marketplace, most products are, more or less, just like their competition. Toilet paper is toilet paper, milk is milk, and a grocery store by any other name is still a grocery store. However, branding takes a product and makes it unique. For example, high-quality drinking water is available from just about every tap in the Western world and it's free, but people pay good money for it when it comes in a bottle. Branding takes bottled water and makes Evian.

Furthermore, every aspect of your brand gives potential customers a feeling or comfort level that they associate with you. The more powerful and positive that feeling is, the more easily and more frequently they will want to do business with you and, indeed, will do business with you.

2. Branding differentiates you from others

Strong branding makes you better than your competition, and makes your product name memorable and easy to remember. Even if your product is absolutely the same as every other product like it, branding makes it special. Branding makes it the first product a consumer thinks about when deciding to make a purchase.

Branding also makes a product seem popular. Everyone knows about it, which implicitly says people like it. And, if people like it, it must be good.

3. Branding makes you worth more money

The stronger your branding is, the more likely people are willing to spend that little bit extra because they believe you, your product, your service, or your business are worth it. They may say they won't, but they will. They do it all the time.

For example, a one-pound box of Godiva chocolates costs about $40; the same weight of Hershey's Kisses costs about $4. The quality of the chocolate isn't ten times greater. The reason people buy Godiva is that the brand Godiva means "gift" whereas the brand Hershey means "snack". Gifts obviously cost more than snacks.

4. Branding pre-sells your product

In the buying age, people most often make the decision on which products to pick up before they walk into the store. The stronger the branding, the more likely people are to think in terms of your product rather than the product category. For example, people are as likely, maybe even more likely, to add Hellmann's to the shopping list as they are to write down simply mayo. The same is true for soda, ketchup, and many other products with successful, strong branding.

Plus, as soon as a shopper gets to the shelf, branding can provide a quick reminder of what products to grab in a few ways:

- An icon or logo
- A specific color
- An audio icon

BRANDING IN A SMALL BUSINESS

Big companies spend millions of dollars on advertising, marketing, and public relations (PR) to build recognition of a new product name. They get their selling messages out to the public using television, radio, magazines, and the Internet. They can even throw money at damage control when necessary. The strategies for branding are the same in a small business, but the scale, costs, and a few of the tactics change.

Make your brand name work harder

The name of a small business can mean everything in terms of branding. Your brand name needs to work harder for your business than you do. It's the first thing a prospective customer sees, and it is how they will remember you. A brand name has to be memorable when spoken, and focused in its meaning. If the name doesn't represent what consumers believe about a product and the company that makes it, then that brand will fail.

In building your product's reputation and image, less is often significantly more. Make sure the name you choose immediately gives a sense of what you do.

Large corporations have millions of dollars to take a meaningless brand name and make it stand for something. Small businesses don't, so use words that really mean something. Strive for something interesting and be right on point. You don't need to be boring.

Plumbers, for example, would do well setting themselves apart with names like "The On-Time Plumber" or "24/7 Plumbing". The same is true for electricians, IT providers, or even marketing consultants. Plenty of other types of business are so general in nature they just don't work hard enough in a business or product name.

Even the playing field: The Net

The Internet has leveled the playing field for small businesses like nothing else. You can use the Internet in several ways to market your brand:

Website: Developing and maintaining a website is easier than ever. Anyone can find your business regardless of its size.

Social Media: Facebook and Twitter can promote your brand in a cost-effective manner.

BUILDING YOUR BRAND WITH THE BRANDING LADDER

Even if you do everything perfectly the first time (and I don't know anyone who does), branding takes time. How much time isn't just up to you, but you can speed things along by understanding the different levels of branding, as well as the business and marketing strategies that can get you to the top.

Introducing the Branding Ladder

Moving through the levels of branding is like climbing a ladder to the top of the marketplace. The Branding Ladder has five distinct rungs and, unlike stairs, you can't take them two at a time. You have to take them in order, and some businesses spend more time on each rung than others.

You can also think of the Branding Ladder in terms of a scale from zero to ten. Everyone starts at zero. If you properly climb the ladder, you can end up at 12 out of 10. The Branding Ladder below shows a special rung at the top of the ladder that can take your business over the top. The following section explains the Branding Ladder and how your small business can move up it.

THE BRANDING LADDER	
Brand Advocacy	12/10
Brand Insistence	10/10
Brand Preference	3/10
Brand Awareness	1/10
Brand Absence	0/10

Rung 1: Living in the void

Your business, in fact every business, starts at the bottom rung, which is called brand absence, meaning you have no brand whatsoever except your own name. On a scale of one to ten, brand absence is, of course, zero. That's the worst place to live and obviously the most difficult entrepreneurially. The good news is that the only way is up.

Ninety-seven percent of businesses live on this rung of the Branding Ladder. They earn far less than they want to earn, far less than they should earn, and far less than they would earn if they did exactly the same work under a real brand.

Rung 2: Achieving awareness

Brand awareness is a good first step up the ladder to the second rung. Actually, it's really good, especially because 97 percent of businesses never get there. You want people to be aware of you. When person A speaks to person B and says, "Have you heard of "The 24/7 Plumber?" You want the answer to be "yes".

On that scale of one to ten, however, brand awareness is only a one. It's better than nothing, but not that much better. Although people know of your brand, being aware doesn't mean that they are interested in buying it. Coca Cola drinkers know about Pepsi, but they don't drink it.

Rung 3: Becoming the preferred brand

Getting to the third rung, brand preference, is definitely a real step up. This rung means that people prefer to use your product or service rather than that of your competition. They believe there is a real difference between you and others, and you're their first choice. This rung is a crucial branding stage for parity products, such as bottled water and breakfast cereals, not to mention plumbers, electricians, lawyers, and all the others. Brand preference is clearly better than brand awareness, but it's less than halfway up the ladder.

Car rental companies represent a perfect example of why brand preference may not be enough. When someone lands at an airport and needs to rent a car on the spot, he or she may go straight to the preferred rental counter. If that company has a car available, it's a sale. However, if all the cars for that company have been rented, the person will move to the next rental kiosk without much thought, because one rental car is just as good as another.

Exerting Brand Preference needs to be easy and convenient

If all you have is brand preference, your business is on shaky ground and you can lose business for the feeblest of reasons. Very few people go to a second or third supermarket just to find their favorite brand of bottled water. Similarly, a shopper may prefer one store over another but, if both stores sell the same products, he or she will often go to the closest store even if it is not the better liked one. The reason for staying nearby does not need to be a dramatic one — the shopper may simply be tired, on a tight schedule, or not in the mood to travel.

Rung 4: Making it you and only you

When your customers are so committed to your product or service that they won't accept a substitute, you have reached the fourth rung of the Branding Ladder. All companies strive to reach this place, called brand insistence.

Brand insistence means that someone's experience with a product in terms of performance, durability, customer service, and image has been sufficiently exceptional. As a result, the product has earned an incredible level of loyalty.

If the product isn't available where the customer is, he or she will literally not buy something else. Rather, the person will look for the preferred product elsewhere. Can you imagine what a fabulous place this is for a company to be? Brand insistence is the best of the best, the perfect ten out of ten, the whole ball of wax.

Apple is a perfect example of brand insistence

Apple users don't just think, they know in their heads and hearts, that anything made by Apple is technologically-advanced, user-friendly, and just all-around superior. Committed to everything Apple, Mac users won't even entertain the thought that a PC may have positive attributes.

Apple people love everything about their Macs, iPads, iPhones, the Mac stores and all those apps. When the company introduces a new product, many of its brand-insistent fans actually wait in line overnight to be one of the first to have it. Steve Jobs is one of their idols.

Considering one big potential problem

Unfortunately, you can lose brand insistence much more quickly than you can achieve it. Brand-insistent customers have such high expectations that they can be disillusioned or disappointed by just one bad product experience. You also have to consistently reinforce the positives because insistence can fade over time. Even someone who has bought and re-bought a specific brand of car for the last 20 years can decide it's just time for a change. That's how fickle the world is.

At ten out of ten, brand insistence may seem like the top rung of the ladder, but it's not. One rung is actually better, and it involves getting your brand-insistent customers to keep polishing your brand for you.

Rung 5: Getting customers to do the work for you

Brand advocacy is the highest rung on the ladder. It's better than ten out of ten because you have customers who are so happy with your product that they want everyone to know about it and use it. Think of them as uber-fans. Not only do they recommend you to friends and family, they also practically shout your praises from the rooftops, interrupt conversations among strangers to give their opinion, and tell everyone they meet how fantastic you are. Most companies can only aspire to this level of customer satisfaction. Apple is one of the few large corporations in recent history that has brand advocates all over the world.

- Brand advocacy does the following five extraordinary things for your company. Brand advocacy:

- Provides a level of visibility that you couldn't pay for if you tried. Brand advocates are so enthusiastic they talk about you all the time, and reach people in ways general media and public relations can't. You get great visibility because they make sure people actually listen.

- Delivers free advertising and public relations. Companies love the extra super-positive messaging, all for free.

- Affords a level of credibility that literally can't be bought. Brand advocates are more than just walking testimonials. They are living proof that you are the best.

- Provides pre-sold prospective customers. Advocate recommendations carry so much weight that they are worth much more than plain referrals. They deliver customers ready and committed to purchasing your product or service.

- Increases profits exponentially. Brand advocates are money-making machines for your business because they increase sales and decrease marketing costs.

For these reasons, brand advocacy is 12 out of 10!!

BRANDING YOURSELF: HOW TO DO SO IN FOUR EASY WAYS

If you're interested in branding your product or company, you may not be sure where to begin. The good news: I'm here to help. You can brand in many ways, but here I pare it down to four ways to help you start:

Branding by association

This way involves hanging out with and being seen with people who are very much higher than you in your particular niche.

Branding by achievement

This way repurposes your previous achievements.

Branding by testimonial

This way makes use of the testimonials that you receive but have likely never used.

Branding by WOW

A WOW is the pleasantly unexpected, the equivalent of going the extra mile. The easiest and most certain way to WOW people is to tell them that you've written a book. To discover how you can write a book of own, go to www.BrandingSmallBusinessForDummies.com.

Happiness: How to Experience the "Real Deal"s

MARCI SHIMOFF

I was 41 years old, stretched out on a lounge chair by my pool and reflecting on my life. I had achieved all that I thought I needed to be happy.

You see, when I was a child, I thought there would be five main things that would ensure that I'd be happy: a successful career helping people, a loving husband, a comfortable home, a great body, and a wonderful circle of friends. After years of study, hard work, and a few "lucky breaks," I finally had them all. (Okay, so my body didn't quite look like Halle Berry's—but four out of five isn't bad!) You think I'd have been on the top of the world.

But surprisingly I wasn't. I felt an emptiness inside that the outer successes of life couldn't fill. I was also afraid that if I lost any of those things, I might be miserable. Sadly, I knew I wasn't alone in feeling this way.

While happiness is the one thing we all truly want, so few people really experience the deep and lasting fulfillment that fills our soul. Why aren't we finding it?

Because, in the words of the old country western song, we're looking for happiness in "all the wrong places."

Looking around, I saw that the happiest people I knew weren't the most successful and famous. Some were married, some were single. Some had lots of money, and some didn't have a dime. Some of them even had health challenges. From where I stood, there seemed to be no rhyme or reason to what made people happy. The obvious question became: *Could a person actually be happy for no reason?*

I had to find out.

So I threw myself into the study of happiness. I interviewed scores of scientists, as well as 100 unconditionally happy people. (I call them the Happy 100.) I delved into the research from the burgeoning field of positive psychology, the study of the positive traits that enable people to enjoy meaningful, fulfilling, and happy lives.

What I found changed my life. To share this knowledge with others, I wrote a book called *Happy for No Reason: 7 Steps to Being Happy from the Inside Out*.

One day, as I sat down to compile my findings, all the pieces of the puzzle fell into place. I had a simple, but profound "a-ha"—there's a continuum of happiness:

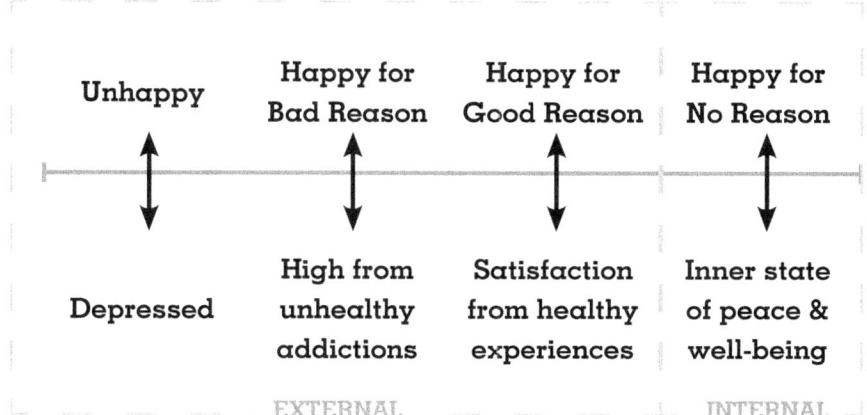

Unhappy: We all know what this means: life seems flat. Some of the signs are anxiety, fatigue, feeling blue or low—your "garden-variety" unhappiness. This isn't the same as clinical depression, which is characterized by deep despair and hopelessness that dramatically interferes with your ability to live a normal life, and for which professional help is absolutely necessary.

Happy for Bad Reason: When people are unhappy, they often try to make themselves feel better by indulging in addictions or behaviors that may feel good in the moment but are ultimately detrimental. They seek the highs that come from drugs, alcohol, excessive sex, "retail therapy," compulsive gambling, over-eating, and too much television-watching, to name a few. This kind of "happiness" is hardly happiness at all. It is only a temporary way to numb or escape our unhappiness through fleeting experiences of pleasure.

Happy for Good Reason: This is what people usually mean by happiness: having good relationships with our family and friends, success in our careers, financial security, a nice house or car, or using our talents and strengths well. It's the pleasure we derive from having the healthy things in our lives that we want.

Don't get me wrong. I'm all for this kind of happiness! It's just that it's only half the story. Being Happy for Good Reason depends on the external conditions of our lives—these conditions change or are lost, our happiness usually goes too. Relying solely on this type of happiness is where a lot of our fear is stemming from these days. We're afraid the things we think we need to be happy may be slipping from our grasp.

Deep inside, I think we all know that life isn't meant to be about getting by, numbing our pain, or having everything "under control." True happiness doesn't come from merely collecting an assortment of happy experiences. At our core, we know there's something more than this.

There is. It's the next level on the happiness continuum—Happy for No Reason.

Happy for No Reason: This is true happiness—a state of peace and well-being that isn't dependent on external circumstances.

Happy for No Reason isn't elation, euphoria, mood spikes, or peak experiences that don't last. It doesn't mean grinning like a fool 24/7 or experiencing a superficial high. Happy for No Reason isn't an emotion. In fact, when you are Happy for No Reason, you can have *any* emotion—including sadness, fear, anger or hurt—but you still experience that underlying state of peace and well-being.

When you're Happy for No Reason, you *bring* happiness to your outer experiences rather than trying to *extract* happiness from them. You don't need to manipulate the world around you to try to make yourself happy. You live from happiness, rather than *for* happiness.

This is a revolutionary concept. Most of us focus on being Happy for Good Reason, stringing together as many happy experiences as we can, like beads in a necklace, to create a happy life. We have to spend a lot of time and energy trying to find just the right beads so we can have a "happy necklace".

Being Happy for No Reason, in our necklace analogy, is like having a happy string. No matter what beads we put on our necklace—good, bad or indifferent—our inner experience, which is the string that runs through them all, is happy, and creates a happy life.

Happy for No Reason is a state that's been spoken of in virtually all spiritual and religious traditions throughout history. The concept is universal. In Buddhism, it is called causeless joy; in Christianity, the kingdom of Heaven within; and in Judaism it is called *ashrei*, an inner sense of holiness and health. In Islam it is called *falah*, happiness and well-being; and in Hinduism it is called *ananda*, or pure bliss. Some traditions refer to it as an enlightened or awakened state.

So how can you be Happy for No Reason?

Science is verifying the way. Researchers in the field of positive psychology have found that we each have a "happiness set-point," that determines our level of happiness. No matter what happens, whether it's something as exhilarating as winning the lottery or as challenging as a horrible accident, most people eventually return to their original happiness level. Like your weight set-point, which keeps the scale hovering around the same number, your happiness set-point will remain the same **unless you make a concerted effort to change it.** In the same way you'd crank up the thermostat to get comfortable on a chilly day, you actually have the power to reprogram your happiness set-point to a higher level of peace and well-being. The secret lies in practicing the habits of happiness.

Some books and programs will tell you that you can simply decide to be happy. They say just make up your mind to be happy—and you will be.

I don't agree.

You can't just decide to be happy, any more than you can decide to be fit or to be a great piano virtuoso and expect instant mastery. You can, however, decide to take the necessary steps, like exercising or taking piano lessons—and by practicing those skills, you can get in shape or give recitals. In the same way, you can become Happy for No Reason through practicing the habits of happy people.

All of your habitual thoughts and behaviors in the past have created specific neural pathways in the wiring in your brain, like grooves in a record. When we think or behave a certain way over and over, the neural pathway is strengthened and the groove becomes deeper—the way a well-traveled route through a field eventually becomes a clear-cut path. Unhappy people tend to have more negative neural pathways. This is why you can't just ignore the realities of your brain's wiring and *decide* to be happy! To raise your level of happiness, you have to create new grooves.

Scientists used to think that once a person reached adulthood, the brain was fairly well "set in stone" and there wasn't much you could do to change it. But new research is revealing exciting information about the brain's neuroplasticity: when you think, feel and act in different ways, the brain changes and actually rewires itself. You aren't doomed to the same negative neural pathways for your whole life. Leading brain researcher Dr. Richard Davidson, of the University of Wisconsin says, "Based on what we know of the plasticity of the brain, we can think of things like happiness and compassion as skills that are no different from learning to play a musical instrument or tennis …. it is possible to train our brains to be happy."

While a few of the Happy 100 I interviewed were born happy, most of them learned to be happy by practicing habits that supported their happiness. That means wherever you are on the happiness continuum, it's entirely in your power to raise your happiness level.

In the course of my research, I uncovered 21 core happiness habits that anyone can use to become happier and stay that way. You can find all 21 happiness habits at www.HappyForNoReason.com

Here are a few tips to get you started:

1. **Incline Your Mind Toward Joy.** Have you noticed that your mind tends to register the negative events in your life more than the positive? If you get ten compliments in a day and one criticism, what do you remember? For most people, it's the criticism. Scientists call this our "negativity bias" — our primitive survival wiring that causes us to pay more attention to the negative than the positive. To reverse this bias, get into the daily habit of consciously registering the positive around you: the sun on your skin, the taste of a favorite food, a smile or kind word from a co-worker or friend. Once you notice something positive, take a moment to savor it deeply and feel it; make it more than just a mental observation. Spend 20 seconds soaking up the happiness you feel.

2. **Let Love Lead.** One way to power up your heart's flow is by sending loving kindness to your friends and family, as well as strangers you pass on the street. Next time you're waiting for the elevator at work, stuck in a line at the store or caught up in traffic, send a silent wish to the people you see for their happiness, well-being, and health. Simply wishing others well switches on the "pump" in your own heart that generates love and creates a strong current of happiness.

3. **Lighten Your Load.** To make a habit of letting go of worries and negative thoughts, start by letting go on the physical level. Cultural anthropologist Angeles Arrien recommends giving or throwing away 27 items a day for nine days. This deceptively simple practice will help you break attachments that no longer serve you.

4. **Make Your Cells Happy.** Your brain contains a veritable pharmacopeia of natural happiness-enhancing neurochemicals — endorphins, serotonin, oxytocin, and dopamine — just waiting to be released to every organ and cell in your body. The way that you eat, move, rest, and even your facial expression can shift the balance of your body's feel-good-chemicals, or "Joy Juice", in your favor. To dispense some extra Joy Juice — smile. Scientists have discovered that smiling decreases stress hormones and boosts happiness chemicals, which increase the body's T-cells, reduce pain, and enhance relaxation. You may not feel like it, but smiling — even artificially to begin with — starts the ball rolling and will turn into a real smile in short order.

5. **Hang with the Happy.** We catch the emotions of those around us just like we catch their colds — it's called emotional contagion. So it's important to make wise choices about the company you keep. Create appropriate boundaries with emotional bullies and "happiness vampires" who suck the life out of you. Develop your happiness "dream team" — a mastermind or support group you meet with regularly to keep you steady on the path of raising your happiness.

"Happily ever after" isn't just for fairytales or for only the lucky few. Imagine experiencing inner peace and well-being as the backdrop for everything else in your life. When you're Happy for No Reason, it's not that your life always looks perfect — it's that, however it looks, you'll still be happy!

By Marci Shimoff. Based on the New York Times bestseller *Happy for No Reason: 7 Steps to Being Happy from the Inside Out*, which offers a revolutionary approach to experiencing deep and lasting happiness. The woman's face of the *Chicken Soup for the Soul* series and a featured teacher in *The Secret*, Marci is an authority on success, happiness, and the law of attraction. To order *Happy for No Reason* and receive free bonus gifts, go to www.happyfornoreason.com/mybook.

Sex, Love and Relationships

DR. JOHN GRAY

Just as great sex is important to lasting love, good health is important to sex and relationships. About 12 years ago, I cured myself of early stage Parkinson's disease. The doctors were amazed, but my wife was even more amazed. She noted that our relationship and sex life had become dramatically better. It turns out that the natural supplements I used to reverse Parkinson's can also make you more attentive and loving in your relationship. At that point, I realized that good relationship skills alone were not enough to sustain love and passion for a lifetime.

I shared many insights gained from my 40 years' experience as a marriage counselor and coach in *Men Are From Mars, Women Are From Venus*. And while my insights go a long way towards helping men and women understand and support each other, good communication skills alone are not always enough. For better relationships, we not only need to be healthy, but we must also experience optimum brain function.

If you are tired, depressed, anxious, not sleeping well, or in pain, then certainly romantic feelings will become a thing of the past. My recovery from Parkinson's revealed to me the profound connection between the quality of our health and our relationships. This insight has motivated me, over the past twelve years, to research the secrets of optimum health as a foundation for lasting love.

These are health secrets that are generally not explored in medical school. In medical school, doctors are indoctrinated into the culture of examining the symptoms, identifying the sickness, and prescribing a drug to treat that sickness. They learn very little about how to be healthy or to sustain successful relationships.

There are no university courses entitled "Better Nutrition For Better Sex". Drugs sometimes save lives, but they also have negative side effects that do little to preserve the passion in a relationship. Ideally, drugs should be used as a last resort and 90 % of our health plan should be drug free. From this perspective, the heath care crisis, as well as our high rate of divorce in America, is indirectly caused by our dependence on doctors and prescription drugs.

Most people have not even considered that taking prescribed drugs (even for the small stuff) can weaken their relationships, which in turn makes them more vulnerable to more disease. For example, if you are feeling depressed or anxious, a drug may numb your pain, but it does nothing to help you correct the cause of your problem. It can even prevent you from feeling your natural motivation to get the emotional support you need. In a variety of ways, our common health complaints are all expressions of two major conditions: our lack of education to identify and support unmet gender-specific emotional needs; and our lack of education to identify and support unmet gender-specific nutritional needs.

With an understanding of natural solutions that have been around for thousands of years, drugs are not needed to treat many common complaints. Some symptoms like low energy, weight gain, allergies, hormonal imbalance, mood swings, poor sleep, indigestion, lack of focus, ADD and ADHD, procrastination, low motivation, memory loss, decreased libido, PMS, vaginal dryness, muscle and joint pain, or the lack of passion in life and/or our relationships can be treated drug-free. By using drugs (even over-the-counter drugs) to treat these common complaints, our bodies and relationships are weakened, making us more vulnerable to bigger and more costly health challenges like cancer, diabetes, heart disease, auto-immune disease, dementia, and Alzheimer's. In simple terms, by handling the easy stuff (the common complaints) without doctors and drugs, we can protect ourselves from the big stuff (cancer, heart disease, dementia, etc.) We can be healthy and also enjoy lasting love and passion in our personal lives.

Even if you are taking anti-depressants or hormone replacement therapy, sometimes all it takes to stop treating the symptom is to directly handle the cause. With specific mineral orotates (something most people have never heard of) or omega three oil from the brains of salmon, your stress levels immediately drop and you begin to feel happy and in love again.

For every health challenge, we have explored the effects on our relationships, with as well as natural remedies that can sometimes produce immediate positive results. You can find these natural solutions to common health complaints for free at my website: www.MarsVenus.com.

What they don't teach in medical school is how to be healthy and happy without the use of drugs or hormone replacement. By refusing drugs and taking responsibility for your health, a wealth of new possibilities can become available to you. We are designed to be healthy and happy, and it is within our reach if we commit to increasing our knowledge.

New research regarding the brain differences in men and women reveals how specific nutritional supplements, combined with gender-specific relationship and self-nurturing skills, can stimulate the hormones of health, happiness and increased energy. Over the past 10 years in my healing center in California, I witnessed how natural solutions coupled with gender-specific relationship skills could solve our common health complaints without drugs. By addressing these common complaints without prescribed drugs, not only do we feel better, but our relationships have the potential to improve dramatically.

Ultimately the cause of all our common complaints is higher stress levels. Researchers around the world all agree that chronic stress levels in our bodies provide a basis for any and all disease to take hold. An easy and quick solution for lowering our stress reactions is specific nutritional support combined with gender-smart relationship skills. Extra nutritional support is needed because stress depletes the body very quickly of essential nutrients. When a car engine is running more quickly, it uses fuel more quickly. When we are stressed, we need both extra nutrients and extra emotional support. Understanding what we need to take and where to get it requires education. Every week day at www.MarsVenus.com I have a live daily show where I freely answer questions and provide this much-needed new gender-specific insight.

At www.MarsVenus.com, we are happy to share what we have learned for creating healthy bodies and positive relationships. You can find a host of natural solutions for common complaints and feel confident that you have the power to feel fully alive with an abundance of energy and positive feelings that will enrich all your relationships.

A Dream Life for the Asking

Tom Barber

There is an enchanting transformation that occurs during those fleeting moments between sleeping and waking as you emerge out of a deep, relaxed slumber before the demands of the day come tumbling into your conscious world. It is also a magical moment of pure potentiality that contains seeds of inspiration or a solution to that insolvable problem that has hounded you for days. Just as you're about to reach out for that breakthrough thought (the one that teeters on the edge of your consciousness), the alarm clock rings, your smartphone dings a text message alert, your baby cries or your dog bays for food. You lose that thread of inspiration; it's gone as if it never existed.

Have you experienced those moments when you say, "But I just had it in my head, it was *right* there!" only to realize that creativity has tenuously slipped through your fingers?

What if you were able to access this state of pure potentiality as often as you wanted to, when you wanted to? You may require some expert assistance in the beginning to reprogram your beliefs so that you know it is, indeed, possible. However, once you've exercised your "mental muscles" and familiarised your mind and body often enough to get the process fully, you will be able to tap into this infinite source of creativity, inspiration, solutions and possibility at will. What if you could access this untapped power for health, greater happiness and contentment, and for peak performance and success, as if it were "second nature"? Well, you can.

Hypnosis is the technology I use to usher people into deep trance states where they can connect to their inner power. Coined by James Braid, a 19th century Scottish surgeon, the term hypnosis comes from "Hypnos," the Greek god of sleep. You don't fall asleep during hypnosis, however; instead you enter a state of deep, calm relaxation during which you can work directly with your subconscious, that part of your mind that takes care of everything behind the scenes.

Back to that moment in the morning, when you're woken up by the barking of your dogs. From that point on, your conscious mind takes over; it goes through the checklist of what you've got to do during the day, the meetings you've got to attend, the chat you're going to have with your boss or travel plans you're going to make for your next vacation. It seems as if the conscious mind is calling the shots, but actually the subconscious mind is continually doing all the hard work.

It is the subconscious that keeps the heart beating, and that tells your lungs to keep pumping oxygen, which speeds up the movement of your legs as a car is threatening to run you down while you are crossing the street. When you cut yourself, you don't think logically to yourself, "Okay, time for the blood to clot now and the white cells to come fight off infection!" All these seemingly simple, yet intricate reactions are silently and efficiently orchestrated by the powerful subconscious. Think of it as your life's Control Panel.

The pure power of the subconscious is revealed in fleeting moments all the time, even when you're asleep. We're just not always aware it's happening. When you've had a stroke of inspiration, or the genius of an idea, that moment of "divine aha!" leaps out like a Jack-in-the-box, released into your conscious mind. The latter is often met, however, with the vast amounts of data, external stimuli, emotions and physical experiences that are part of your interaction with the world from moment to moment. The trick is to keep the genius intact and to expand its reality within your conscious world. You can learn how to do that too.

The subconscious is the seat of imagination, impulse, creativity and emotion and is also the storehouse of your memories, which means it's one mighty big reservoir. Tapping into it at will and harnessing its power can be truly awesome.

SO WHAT DOES IT ALL MEAN?

What does all this have to do with hypnosis? How can it reveal to us such inner power? Hypnosis takes you to that relaxed state, where your brain frequency literally slows down. Your subconscious mind can then come to the front of the stage as the headline act and revel in the spotlight. In a hypnotic trance state, you remain alert, but you're incredibly focused, just as if you were fully engaged in a really good book or a compelling movie. You switch off external stimuli and are fully engaged in the world of the book or film as if you were right there, in the story.

Hypnosis gives you the key to open the door to the subconscious, access its amazing wealth of information, creativity and resources. It allows you to "anchor" a positive mindset and feelings to be accessed at any point in the future. In this manner, you gain distinct control of your emotions and can manage your mindset for positive behaviour, essentially creating the outcomes you've only ever dreamed of before.

Let's take an example. Let's say you almost drowned when you were a little kid and have since avoided the water. Now an adult, every time you approach the sea, you have a plunging feeling in your stomach. You feel left out on beach holidays because you're afraid of being too close to the water; you don't even dip a toe in the swimming pool. However, you've fallen in love with a marine biologist and you feel that there's something missing if you can't share the love of being in the water with your new partner. Are you always going to stay on the sidelines, or are you going to engage with life so you can have endless fun and build great memories with the love of your life? Which would you choose?

You've been dominated by fear surrounding the bad experience but, with hypnosis, I can take away the sting of the anxiety and terror, as well as any undesirable thoughts that creep into your mind unwillingly at the sight of the ocean. Then, I can help you replace those unhappy memories with a new, more desirable set of emotions and sensory experiences. I can explore with you any feelings of fun, delight and sharing that you've encountered previously in doing something else, like playing football or cooking with friends, and link those feelings with being in the water. By taking these steps, we would together reprogram your mind-body connection so that it reacts positively to swimming and everything associated with it, such as soaking up the warm sun, feeling the breeze, tasting the salt in the water, thriving in the adventure and, ultimately, enjoying more intimate love!

To ensure you can re-access this desirable state, I use a technique called Clenched Fist Auto Anchoring to make sure that these positive emotions are powerfully stored in your body's memory. By anchoring this sensory experience and all its powerfully positive benefits that are meaningful to *you*, it ensures that you can retrieve or spark happy feelings and sensations around water any time you want, in any situation, at will.

Together, through hypnosis, we will have moved you from a previously inhibiting fear to a pleasurable and fearless sense of freedom and adventure. Your whole world will have just changed immeasurably. This is just one example of how well hypnosis works; it is effective in all situations, from helping you pass your driving exam to overcoming your anxiety around public speaking to surmounting weight problems, habits and low-esteem, to finding your life's purpose and creating great success beyond your wildest dreams.

BELIEVE YOU DESERVE MORE, GET MORE

Hypnotherapy is a powerful technology, and it changes lives. The first step forward begins with *you*.

Ask yourself…
- Do you feel that your life could be better lived?
- Do you long to contribute more positively to your family, your friends, your customers and to the world at large?
- Do you feel frustrated because you don't know which direction to take?

- Are you just plain stuck and unwilling to get out of the hole?
- Do you feel there's a vision inside you waiting to be birthed, but you don't know what it is?

The good news is that you'll never have to live another day feeling "less than" or empty, or thinking you're incompetent, unworthy or undeserving. As long as you believe that positive change is possible, that you deserve more than what you're getting right now and that you are capable of great achievements and deeds, positive change is not only possible, it's yours for the taking. What you need now is *the how*.

Hypnosis addresses that "how," that all-important nourishing factor that creates the changes you desire. It's not "if" you can change, but "how" we are going to do this. In my 20 years of experience as a highly qualified psychotherapist using hypnosis and Neuro-Linguistic Programming (NLP), and through my continuing studying and questing, I've found what I believe to be the essential essence that creates the magical moment of true potential where the hypnotic transformation can effortlessly evolve.

The key lies with the ability of one human being to connect with another as well as being deeply attuned to the knowledge and skills inextricably linked to the hypnotic encounter. This is what allows me to connect to the remarkable depth of experience and human-ness of the person who sits by my side. It's about having a true desire to guide you simply through your journey of change, fully believing you can change, even when, right in that moment, your belief is wavering.

Your connection and trust *will* shape and influence the depth of inner journeying, the quality of your therapist's language *will* impact the speed at which you arrive at your desirable state of being, and his or her ultimate belief and faith that change is yours for the taking will impact your ability to access these positive experiences in the future. This I have seen many, many times.

Within myself, I have uncovered the ability to create deep levels of connection with my clients at lightning fast speed, allowing change to happen seamlessly, where extraordinary shifts are open for those who want to achieve, with definitively measurable results. Through my work with many thousands of clients and students, I have harnessed an ability to quickly "feel' where someone is at, to understand how to navigate around their inner terrain and to engage their trust. This ignites their own belief that they can change and really take back control of their futures. I completely believe that change is yours for the taking if you are doing the asking. It is this belief that shines through and creates formidable levels of expectation. When this is in place, the path to change is fully open to the methods and techniques of *how*.

I've been privileged to share amazing transformations as I've delivered conferences and workshops around the world in places such as Eastern Europe, China, Russia and Mexico, all via an interpreter. It's truly phenomenal to experience the depth of the human connection that comes to the fore when words no longer offer a possible means of instant communication, creating a profound and unforgettably moving experience as inner change unfolds before our very eyes.

Such learning has really equipped me to *know* how to move past the words of a story to the deep, true thoughts and feelings of another human being longing for things to change. No two clients are the same, so there's no cookie-cutter approach, but I believe in some fundamentals to embody, some skills that crucially lead the way alongside the "how" for this particular, unique human being with more potential than he or she yet knows. And that's my wonderful job, my life and my inspiration!

My passion for healing others, and my unwavering exploration into my world as my own journey unfolds, places me in the unique position of travelling the path that will need to be walked for this journey of life to evolve further for you too. I've climbed the mountain before, and I know the track well, so I can guide the people I work with from where they are now to where they want to be. And, if they aren't sure about where that is, I can help them locate just what that destination point is too.

My decision to become a therapist fanned an inner flame, which I hadn't known existed, to learn the art of helping others and changing lives. As I engaged in helping others, I found that I tapped into another joy, learning the depths of myself, discovering my inner undiscovered dimensions, becoming freer and more engaged with life and my healing practices. And so the journey continues to unfold.

LIVING A LIFE TO BE PROUD OF

Those are some of the benefits I would like to pass on to you. You see, there is so much that we can do … and so much that you can do too. You can learn to self-hypnotise for those times when you have no access to a trained therapist, so you can harness your tremendous personal power and live a life of which you are proud.

You might be surprised to discover that you *already* self-hypnotise. We all do. Driving to work and being oblivious of your journey, watching TV and losing track of the plot, finding yourself daydreaming out of the office window. These are all examples of drifting into a state of hypnosis. Imagine learning what you can do with that!

Think about the customs that sports teams go through before a big game – the pre-game rituals and the pep talks that are meant to pump up the team and strike fear in the hearts of the opponents.

In the formidable game of rugby, my all-time passion, the New Zealand All Blacks like to take the temperature up a notch and intimidate the competition by performing the Haka, the traditional Maori dance. It involves loud war cries, heavy pounding of feet, stylised gestures of violence, fierce facial expressions with hanging tongues and glowering stares, all barely feet away from the competing team. Yet, the purpose is not just to frighten off the opposing players; the gestures and stomping are a means of "hypnotising" themselves into states where they are strong, fierce and powerful. It is a means by which they tap into the legendary courage of the Maori warriors of old.

So, a dream life is yours for the asking. If you believe you can have an expanded life with more creativity, more accomplishments, more freedom and more passion, if you believe you can be more aligned, the "how" is right there in your hands. It really is within your reach and your grasp. I invite you to walk the path with me, and would be honoured to be your companion in growth.

Once Tom Barber discovered hypnotherapy, he found himself reinvigorated and re-engaged with life, soon desiring to help others as he was himself helped. He has become a leading Hypnotherapist and Psychotherapist helping people to make changes they so desperately want and can have through hypnosis.

Tom is an international instructor and in-demand Speaker, and is the award winning author of *The Book on Back Pain: The Ultimate Guide to Permanent Relief*, *The Change Sequence*, and Co-author of *Thinking Therapeutically: Hypnotic Skills and Strategies Explored*. Additionally, he is a Director at Contemporary College of Therapeutic Studies UK, where he trains others also wanting to embark on an enriching and fulfilling career in making a difference to others' lives, whilst also co-ordinating SelfHelpSchool™, which provides Self Help through education for the public. Tom, who is known as 'The Changeologist', consults 'leading lights' in the arenas of sport, art and music, as well as the corporate world, all who are committed to inspirational change and growth strategies using the power of the mind. You can contact Tom at Change@TomBarber.co.uk

Downsize Into a Better, More Fulfilling Rest of Your Life

7 Keys to Preparing for a Great and Rightsize Retirement

Monika Lowry & Robert Miller

Baby Boomers (Zoomers) are retiring, or getting ready to retire, in record numbers. Whether you have carefully set aside a nest egg, or been unable to prepare financially until now, it's crucial that you start to plan ahead today. That's true even if you have already stopped working, because it is likely that you are healthy enough to be retired for as many or more years than you worked.

A "Downsizing Plan" can get you where you want to be. It can help you decide what things you no longer want or need in your life and free you to enjoy those things you've always wanted to do or have. Downsizing need not be a discouraging experience. In fact, having a plan will allow you a new sense of freedom and purpose.

Whether you hope to start your new chapter of life at 55, 64 or even 75, it's to your advantage to start preparing your Downsizing Plan now, while you can have significant control about what your future lifestyle will be. Remember it's choice, not chance, that determines everything that happens in your future. It is a choice to accept responsibility for what happens to you, and to respond to life's challenges with courage and commitment. The alternative is choosing to be a victim, which you obviously don't want to be.

Plus, no matter how carefully you've planned so far, there are bound to be unforeseen circumstances to be addressed moving forward. Changes in health, employment status, accidents and other emergencies can create disruptions and require changes to your Downsizing Plan. But, you can handle whatever comes and still make the next chapter of your life simpler and more enjoyable if you downsize in the right way:

- Start the planning process while still in your working years.

- Determine what major purchases (sunshine condo, sailboat or motor home) will be required to make your retirement a reality and start putting away funds or begin curtailing your current lifestyle to help support tomorrow's dream one. Remember that you're not just cutting expenses; you are ensuring your future.

- Make necessary changes to your Downsizing Plan to handle unexpected events, then regroup and recommit to your planning process.

- Don't dwell on the negative. While it is important to remain realistic, you can have an optimistic attitude. Optimism is a powerful tool that can enable you to make the best of what you have and accomplish your goals. Planning helps you focus on the things that you really want, so you don't miss anything you decide to give away. Don't allow your perspective to be shaped by the fearful stories you hear in the media, or the negativity of others.

SEVEN KEYS TO ACHIEVING THE RETIREMENT YOU DESIRE

Everyone's planning process will vary according to their goals and desires, as well as their current circumstances, but there are seven overall keys to making yourself ready for the next chapter of your life.

1. Downsizing is a process, not an event.

Downsizing is a process of midlife re-engineering, a time of transition from your job or business and your children to that coveted "next chapter" of life you have long anticipated. It means different things to different people … their house, the size of their property, how much of a mortgage they are willing and able to carry forward, their personal health and the things (both material and immaterial) they've accumulated—some of which they may not even be aware they have. You may find it extremely helpful not to think about downsizing, but view at least some of your possibilities as Rightsizing or Shifting Gears.

- Rightsizing looks at hopes and aspirations. Many people put their aspirations on hold and wait until their career and children's education are completed. Only then do they allow themselves the luxury of considering these things for themselves. If this describes you, then you may be a rightsizer.

- Shifting Gears is typically a midlife or pre-retirement strategy. It may be the decision to buy a business, change careers, or step away from a high-profile political or corporate role to devote more time to one's family or health. Whether shifting gears is a proactive choice or a response to changes in your personal health, career or business, it's advisable to seek sound advice and ongoing coaching (more about coaching later in this chapter), and to plan carefully in order to ensure success in your new endeavor.

2. Downsizing encompasses more than your home.

Your home is probably your largest asset, and how it fits in your future lifestyle is a crucial consideration. But, as you've probably already guessed, downsizing is about more than just emptying closets or buying that smaller retirement home! It may include eliminating luxury purchases, sharing one car instead of having two, and finding a retirement job or saving up to open the business you've always wanted to run.

Downsizing can also be about dealing with boomerang children (often with children of their own) who have returned to the nest out of 'short-term' necessity or making other arrangements for parents for whom you've been the primary caregiver. This is never an easy choice, but it is yours. And, you are not the only one facing some tough decisions as many Baby Boomers, whether by culture or choice, are truly part of the "Sandwich Generation." Should you choose to delay the start of your "next chapter," remember that it is your choice. This is just one example of how the unanticipated can result in taking a step back and adjusting your retirement plan to accommodate circumstances.

For those who have been "married to their careers," downsizing may mean letting go of responsibility at the executive level, cutting back on hours or finally starting to take some of those vacations you never had time for. In this case, downsizing is definitely a process, a transitional period to make those changes easier.

3. Downsizing is about "moving on" versus "hanging on."

As Kris Kristofferson said in his hit song "Me and Bobby McGee," "freedom's just another word for nothing left to lose." Alternatively, for downsizers, freedom's just another word for nothing left to get rid of! However, finding that freedom requires the courage and discipline to "let go." Like going to a spa, downsizing is a "cleanse" that allows us to do some "spring cleaning" in our life, home, relationships and business environment. It is essential to stop and assess our achievements and failures, our health and wellbeing, our financial goals and current status. Only by recognizing where we are starting from can we develop a plan and measure our progress against it.

Downsizing can be the positive catalyst that gets you out of a midlife rut. When life becomes too routine, too predictable or mundane, you are at risk of losing your passion—and without passion for what you're doing, you can lose your sense of purpose. This is the time to decide if you really are your career or would rather be working on that novel you always wanted to write.

When it comes to material possessions, you may find that you are holding on to things that no longer have a purpose in your life because you once had an emotional attachment to them. Or, you may be more than ready to pack up those great memories made in your big suburban home and take them to a wonderful condo by the beach, where you never have to mow the lawn or shovel snow again. If you find yourself holding on to your old "stuff," you may find it helpful to remember that it is only by letting go that you can move on. Perhaps the catalyst for your downsizing process is the realization that you could start that small business you always dreamed of if you let go of some of your other "stuff."

Like a major birthday or anniversary, downsizing is a reason to pause, reminisce, share, celebrate, and then move on.

4. Downsizing is a team sport.

Preparing for the next chapter of your life is the start of a major life event, and it is essential you think in terms of "we", not "I." Your planning should involve collaboration with your spouse or partner to determine your individual and shared goals, expectations and priorities. Consider this question: What one shared experience would be the memory of a lifetime if you achieved it together? Successful relationships almost always include at least one shared project the partners are working on and looking forward to, together." It is important to create a joint "bucket list" and plan to do the things important to both of you first so that you can experience them together.

Flagging marriages and tired relationships may be starving for a common goal that both partners can be passionate about. Perhaps you really wanted to spend your February honeymoon in Hawaii, but due to lack of funds you settled for Niagara Falls. Maybe Maui and Kauai are just what you need to make the downsizing process urgent, important and worth doing now. Who knows, once you visit you may decide to move there permanently. (It's expensive, but lots of people are retiring there.)

Planning for both of you is not always an easy task and, probably, each of you will need to compromise. Couples who have already been through this process can provide insight and encouragement to those struggling with this transition, and their experiences are shared at: www.TheBookonDownsizing.com.

You and your spouse or partner need not try to do this on your own. Trying to downsize in a vacuum, with no outside input, can make the process much more daunting, if not impossible, for many people. Even together with your partner, dealing with all of the emotions and micro-decisions necessary to keep the process moving smoothly can be a challenge.

You would be wise to put together a support team to assist you; pick its members carefully, starting with a retirement coach, especially one with expertise in real estate. As you'll soon see, finding the right environment for the next chapter of your life requires a lot of thinking and decision making, including where and what type (rental, condo, attached, apartment or house etc.) of living arrangement you require. For free resources or to learn more about retirement coaches and how to choose the right one for you visit www.TheBookonDownsizing.com.

5. Downsizing starts with simple planning.

As said earlier in this chapter, "Life happens" and we can suddenly be confronted with the necessity to act quickly, without the benefit of time, adequate discussion between spouses, or a defined plan. Unfortunately, this happens to older couples far too frequently, and it can be especially traumatic when one partner, or the family, is faced with the task of sorting through a lifetime of "stuff," including nice furniture and collectibles, not to mention memorabilia, and finding no recipients who would appreciate receiving it.

Whether the individual has passed, or now needs more care than can be provided in their current home, the result is a difficult transition, with unhappiness ebbing all around. In the latter case, the partner who has to leave the home may feel significant guilt for not having acted sooner. The other partner is typically overwhelmed and frustrated by their emotional and physical inability to cope with the task ahead, and the family has to put their own lives on hold to take on this additional responsibility.

In the end, the message is simply "when we fail to plan, we plan to fail." As a result, if we do not proactively develop our plan, however modest, enroll the help of our family or coaches and take action, then the result will be much more difficult than necessary.

6. Downsizing is an exciting journey.

There is seldom a person who, when asked, cannot volunteer at least one thing they really wanted to do in their life, but never got to it. Life happened, and time passed, until the opportunity no longer seemed achievable or important. Don't let this happen to you!

Retirement and downsizing are two enablers that can free you to have the time, the resources, and the opportunity to pursue any dream you ever had. However, without planning, you risk letting time, health and mobility rob you of the chance to fulfill even one of the great adventures life holds for you.

7. Downsizing requires action — just do it!

If you don't already have one, start your bucket list today. That will motivate you to get the discussion going with your spouse or partner. Listen to each other's dreams and spend some time imagining your perfect "together" retirement. Examine your financial health to get a feel for what may be necessary to get you where you want to go. Then, look for a specialized coach, again especially one with real estate expertise, and you will be well on your way.

Have More Money, More Clients and More Freedom by Going Digital

Ashar Alam

As a savvy business owner, you understand that, whatever field you are in, whether it is chiropractic or real estate or Italian food, you are also in the business of marketing. You also know that the key to building and maintaining a successful business lies in keeping your marketing current and effective.

Many traditional forms of marketing simply don't measure up to the digital resources available today. If you haven't embraced this medium yet, you probably have seen competitors who do have a solid digital marketing strategy surging ahead of the pack (that includes you). If your market doesn't have a digital player yet, you have a golden opportunity to leave your competitors behind.

There are several steps you need to take to bring your business digitally up to par, and to get in position to set yourself apart. This chapter of The Authorities will focus on one very powerful digital marketing tool, search engine optimization (usually referred to as SEO). But, first, here's a broad look at exactly what digital marketing is.

DIGITAL MARKETING AUDIT

There are several different questions you should ask yourself in order to assess the current state of your business with respect to digital marketing. The most basic of these is: Do I have a website? If the answer is no, then you need to get one! This is as basic as it gets, but also as essential as it gets. A business's website is really the source from which all other digital marketing strategies flow.

If you do already have a business website, you can pat yourself on the back, but you are not out of the woods yet, not by a long shot. Begin to take a look at how well your site is serving your business:

- **Look critically at your site's URL/domain name.** A domain name like LocksmithSanDiego.com will have a leg up on competitors because it aligns well with what prospects for that business would be searching for on the web. It's also important to realize that a ".com" — or country-specific domains like ".ca" and ".co.uk" — is generally favored most by search engines and looked at as most legitimate by prospects.

- **Think about keywords that are relevant to your business from a customer's perspective.** Consider your own habits. What would you type into a search engine if you were looking for service in your field? The better optimized for these keywords your site is, the easier it will be for your prospects to find it.

- **Do some research to determine where your site ranks on popular search engines.** There is software that will do this, but it is simpler to do a Google search using likely keywords for your business. Does your site come up in the first page of results? The second? Again, think about how you use Google. How often do you navigate past the first or second page of search results? Most Googlers won't get too far past the first several results on the first page which, of course, is where you want your site to be. Optimized SEO can help make that happen.

- **How well does your site work when your prospects actually get there?** Can customers buy your product(s) directly from your website? If so, do they buy from you when they visit your website? How much time do they spend on your site once they get there? You can monitor these statistics, as well as other important website performance factors, with resources like Google Analytics; doing so is essential to getting the most out of your website.

- **Do you take advantage of other digital media channels**, such as social media (Facebook, Twitter, etc.), large retailers (Amazon, iTunes, etc.), mobile apps, and SMS marketing?

These questions and considerations represent a good starting point for assessing your business's digital marketing prowess, but they are really just scratching the surface. There are many more things to look into, whether it's calculating return on investment by estimating the lifetime value of your clients, setting up an infrastructure for capturing clients' email addresses and phone numbers, or optimizing your website for mobile devices.

It might seem like a lot to think about, and it is, but the more you apply these principles to your marketing strategy, the more your business will benefit. Everyone knows that putting in the effort is necessary to bringing about the desired result; what the above guidelines do is help you channel that effort strategically and productively.

SEO

Speaking of using your effort wisely, one of the most important aspects of digital marketing is SEO. You will definitely want to funnel some of your digital marketing efforts into SEO to ensure that your prospects have the opportunity to find out about your business.

The name "search engine optimization" is fairly self-explanatory — it refers to optimizing a website so that it's easy for a search engine to find it. However, properly executing this concept is not as simple as the concept itself is. Keywords, like the ones discussed above, must be well-integrated into the very coding of the various pages on your site. There are also several other factors, such as back links, social markers and likability — discussed in further detail below — that contribute to how your site will fare on the search engines.

Crucially, all of this must be done in a strategic way. Obviously catering to keywords can lead to negative repercussions. Search engines will take action against those who blatantly game the system, banishing them to obscure sections of search results and dealing a severe blow to their digital marketing schemes.

"FREE" ADVERTISING

In the sense that it requires time and effort, and potentially the paid help of a specialist, SEO is not free. However, compared to the level of paid advertising you would have to employ to get the same level of visibility, SEO is a terrific bargain. And, it generates a very strong return on investment (ROI).

In terms of search engines, organic SEO can actually be much more valuable than paid advertising, even without considering cost. The major search engines — Google, Yahoo! and Bing — display unpaid listings on the same results page as paid ones. Plus, local business results are typically included with national ones. Most of the time, web users simply ignore the paid listings, which display on a different part of the page —either off to the side or above the organic listings. (Again, think about your own behavior in such situations — you may have never even noticed that Google displays paid listings alongside the unpaid ones you naturally look for.)

People rely on search engines to provide something like an unbiased survey of what's out there, and paid ads don't fit very well into this expectation. On the other hand, a "real" listing that pops up prominently in the results is more appealing. Websites that pop up toward the beginning of the results do so because they are well optimized for search engines. This is the key to SEO. The effort required is invisible to the customer, and a prominent search engine result comes with built-in legitimacy.

WHAT ARE SEARCH RESULTS BASED ON?

You've already seen how SEO starts with keywords. Your search engine ranking will partly be dependent upon where these keywords show up on your site and how much competition there is for the keywords you target. As a general guideline, strategically placed keywords should not exceed 1-2% of the copy on your site.

"Longtail" keywords, such as "best DUI attorney in Buffalo New York," can help sites succeed in a competitive market, although incorporating them will probably require outside help; for example, from a specialty marketing firm. Because SEO is so important these days, many firms specialize in assisting companies in this way. This is, of course, an extra expense — as discussed above, good SEO is not free — but for many markets its benefits will hugely outweigh the costs.

A more stripped down way to achieve something similar is to incorporate a blog into your website. Blogs continually generate fresh, keyword-rich content, and can help drive traffic to your website. For many businesses, generating blog posts is a more doable in-house operation for enhancing SEO, although it is also something that can be outsourced, and typically for a much lower price than that of hiring a marketing firm.

There are other specific attributes besides keywords that are important as well. Some of these are still intimately related to keywords, while others are completely separate. Google will determine rankings according to:

Authority – How authoritative is a given site in relation to the search term? Has it been highly ranked in the results of this search term for a long time?

Relevance – How popular is this search? Is it generating a lot of web traffic? Are many people searching for these specific keywords?

Competition – What sites mention these keywords? What sites prominently feature these keywords (i.e., in the title or domain name)? What are the SEO-related qualities, both on-page and off-page, of these sites? For example, age, rank, back links (see next bullet point), and prominence and density of keywords.

Back links – These are like citations in an article, and function somewhat as votes for a site. How many other sites are linking back to a given page? Are the sites that are linking to the page in question themselves high-SEO sites? Poor quality back links can be worse than no links at all, as this is exactly the type of thing Google cracks down on. Spammy back links can cause a site to be thrown into the Google "sandbox," meaning it is dropped from the top hundred search results.

Social markers – Does this site have connections with social media sites like Facebook, Twitter and LinkedIn? Are users linking back to it on these platforms?

Likability – Many different measures determine the likability of a site, such as:

- Time spent on page – How long do visitors to a given page stay there before navigating away? Videos are a great way to increase visitors' time spent on your site. A live chat feature is another way to keep visitors from navigating away from a page.

- Bounce rate – The percentage of visitors who leave the site rather than navigate to other pages within the site. A high bounce rate means people who visit your site are not finding a reason to stay there.

- Scroll rate – Do visitors scroll down through a page, or leave directly after it loads without scrolling through? Make sure each page has enough content to engage a visitor. Most pages should have a minimum of 500 words. Meeting that word limit is one easy way to address this issue.

- Grammar – Poor grammar can be a marker of regurgitated content. Sites with high likability will not have grammatical errors.

- Downloads – A great way to increase likability of a page. Offering PDF documents, MP3s, and/or video files as downloads helps to engage visitors to your site.

SEO is certainly a multi-layered topic, and the larger world of digital marketing is even more intensive. This chapter has given you several simple action steps you should take immediately to better market your business online. To learn more about how digital marketing can build your business significantly, you may want to visit thebookondigitalmarketing.com.

In the meantime, look back through the audit above, and through the bulleted list of SEO principles. Satisfactorily dealing with these various aspects of digital marketing is often an ongoing project for successful businesses. There are many angles from which to approach it, which means finding a place to dive in is easy — there are so many options.

SEO in particular is a long term consideration. Working your way into a favorable spot in search engine rankings can take time. But, as discussed above, truly earning a prominent organic listing is highly valuable exposure for a business, so it's a worthy goal to pursue.

And, now that you have some valuable information about how to go about it, go out and spread the word about your business!

Create the Life of Your Dreams

The Savvy Investor's Ultimate Guide to Wholesaling Real Estate

Dexter Montgomery & Pamela Montgomery

Many people look to real estate investment as an enjoyable, flexible, and dependable way to generate income. Whether that means supplementing a day job or completely transforming the way you spend your time and fund your lifestyle, you might be one of these people. Even in a changing housing market, real estate continues to represent an essential part of the economy – neighborhoods transition, young people grow up, properties continue to be bought and sold; great deals are always out there.

The allures of investing in real estate are many – being your own boss, making your own hours, earning more than you ever have before, setting your own financial goals and having the means to meet them – but, while it can be extremely rewarding, entering into real estate can also be very challenging.

The inexperienced will not know the many ins and outs of buying, selling, renting, and rehabbing properties: everything from the appropriate lingo (a must if you want to be taken seriously) to housing market trends and the function of different specialists with whom you must work to be successful. That doesn't even include general entrepreneurial skills like setting goals and educating yourself; these things are absolutely essential to success in real estate investment as well.

As in many other fields, experience can be invaluable in investment, but knowing the lay of the land before you ever get your feet wet is essential. The process of trial and error is not so desirable when an "error" means losing a substantial portion of a large amount of money you have invested.

If you are serious about establishing a career or side-career in real estate investment, you will most certainly make mistakes and experience hardships along the way and, if you are patient and resilient, you will learn from them. However, you have to put the time and effort in before you get involved to ensure that you know what you're doing.

Real estate coaches and seminar speakers will often talk about all the mistakes they made when they were starting out. In this field, that means losing money, sometimes a lot of it. Consider yourself lucky to have the option of using their advice and expertise to help you avoid these same mistakes. Some of this information is free, but immersing yourself in the necessary knowledge will require an investment. You must trust that, if you find the right programs, seminars, coaches, books, and other resources, it is worth every penny.

You will not get to where you need to be by reading one chapter on the subject, but it's a great start. If you're serious about pursuing this opportunity that you know can make your life better and help you realize your goals, you will use a resource like this chapter as a diving board into the "deep end," so to speak, where you can really educate and immerse yourself.

FORMS OF REAL ESTATE INVESTMENT

On a basic level, a big part of diving into real estate investment is a decision about what form of investment to pursue. Eventually, as you grow with your business, you might very well want to expand your efforts, trying different types of investments and determining which ones make the most sense for you and for different types of situations. However, when you are just starting, it is important not to overextend yourself. You will do well to focus on only one type of investment.

What really differentiates one kind of real estate investment from another is the "exit strategy" for a given property. If you think of your initial acquisition of the property as your "entrance," and your plans for that property as your "exit," you begin to see that there are many different options. Planning your exit strategy before you acquire a property is essential to understanding how you will profit from the transaction.

These are the most common ways to profit from a real estate investment:

- **Wholesale**: Acquiring a property at a favorable price from a motivated seller and quickly reselling it to a motivated buyer. You might be selling the property to someone who will then pursue one of the following strategies.

- **Rental**: Acquiring a property and holding on to it for the long term, earning profit on it by leasing to a tenant.

- **Rehab**: Also known as "flipping" a property. It's more of a long term project than wholesale buying and selling. Rehabbing involves acquiring a distressed property and fixing it up to bring up its value, then reselling it.

These various forms of investment differ in several ways, from timeline to resources required to marketplace appropriateness, and many more. A certain property may be better suited to one of these investment methods than to the others. Comparing your expected costs to your expected income will help you decide which is most appropriate.

For example, rehabbing a property balances the combined cost of acquiring it and bringing it back to life against what someone will pay you for it once you've done so. Renting is only prudent when you know the income from your tenant will cover your costs – that includes acquiring, holding, and maintaining the property.

If you intend to wholesale a property, you must have a good understanding of how quickly you can expect to sell it, and at what price. Simply holding on to a property will be one of your costs, due to property tax, so how quickly you sell will determine how much you can profit from that sale. Likewise, buying and reselling a property will, of course, only be profitable to you if your sell price is higher than your buy price. Researching comparable sales, both from a timing and a pricing perspective, will help give you a read on this. The better you know the neighborhood you're buying and selling in, the better you can understand what to expect.

Other factors to consider, both when deciding between types of investment and when determining whether or not to buy in at all, include:

- **Financial risk**: How much are you willing to take on?

- **ROI** (Return on Investment): How much money do you expect to make from this deal, and how quickly do you expect to make it?

- **Your time**: How much time will you have to research the deal? How much time will you have to devote to managing/fixing up/appraising/marketing the property?

- **Your effort**: How much effort are you willing to put into the above considerations?

- **Financing**: Where will the money you are investing come from?

WHOLESALING

As discussed above, dipping your toes into the water of real estate development is a great place to start but, if you're serious about pursuing it, you will eventually dive in all the way. The rest of this chapter will discuss in greater detail one specific facet of real estate investment: wholesaling. You'll want to continue to seek out additional resources to get deeper into the others.

Wholesaling is a great entry point because getting into it doesn't require as much money up front as some of the other types of investment do. As mentioned above, a wholesaler is essentially a "middle man" between a motivated buyer and a motivated seller. Let's dig a little deeper into who these people are and how they are relevant to you, the investor.

Motivated Buyers

To those without a lot of real estate experience, the idea of a property buyer might bring to mind a family buying a home, or a business owner buying a commercial space to use as a storefront or office. Images in media or perhaps from personal experience probably bring to mind buyers concerned about location, and looking for a space they will "fall in love with." You might picture a couple that wants space to raise children and access to good schools, or a store owner looking for an area with good visibility and ample room for storage.

Although these kinds of things are important to certain types of real estate deals, they are not so relevant to the wholesaler. The family and the business owner would not be examples of motivated buyers. Rather, a motivated buyer is someone with ready access to cash, looking for a good investment him- or herself. A motivated buyer will "fall in love" with a property if the numbers indicate that it represents a good business deal.

Finding and attracting these motivated buyers becomes much easier when you are offering them an attractive price. This is why understanding the market is so important in a wholesale deal. You have to be sure that, when you buy a property, you will be able to resell it at a price that is low enough to easily and quickly attract motivated buyers and high enough to provide you with a profit.

Offering great deals to motivated buyers – and handling transactions professionally and ethically – will encourage those buyers to come back to you again and again, looking for more opportunities to buy from you. As your business grows, you can begin to put together a database of names and build a network.

In fact, networks of this kind already exist in many forms, and getting access to them is a great first step to finding motivated buyers. Joining a local real estate investment club is one way to meet other investors and begin to build your network. You can also meet investors by attending property auctions. Networking in this way is an invaluable part of getting started in property wholesaling.

Motivated Sellers

Let's talk about the other side of the equation, the motivated seller. Just as a motivated buyer is someone with cash in hand, looking to buy quickly, rather than someone carefully searching for a property to "fall in love with," a motivated seller is not somebody who would like to sell a property, or is maybe considering it, but somebody who has to sell, for one reason or another.

A motivated seller will have a strong reason (usually a financial one) compelling him or her to sell. Falling behind on a mortgage, suffering a personal hardship like divorce or loss of a job, and inheriting an unwanted property are examples. As a wholesaler, you are in a position to solve a problem for a motivated seller. You can take a property off the seller's hands and move it to someone who wants it.

In this way, real estate wholesaling is really a win-win-win situation. The seller gets rid of an unwanted or unsustainable property, the buyer finds a good investment and you, the wholesaler, essentially earn a fee for bringing these two parties together. You might think of this as a sort of "finder's fee."

So how do you find these motivated sellers? There are several different strategies you might consider. These sellers have to know that you are available to provide them with this service, so marketing yourself is essential.

Advertising is an important way to get onto a potential seller's radar, be it through the newspaper, the internet, or even a sign along the road.

You can also proactively look for properties by combing through listings or by driving or walking around in an area and hunting for "For Sale" signs. When physically going around and looking at properties, seek out distressed or vacant homes and "FSBO" (For Sale by Owner) signs. While searching through listings, keep an eye out for expiring listings and those labeled things like "Handyman Special" or "Needs Work".

Here again, networking can come in handy, as working with real estate agents who search the MLS (Multiple Listing Service) can give you access to these types of listings. Another group, sometimes known as "bird dogs," can be a great resource too. Bird dogs are people who pass on good deals to wholesalers, for a fee. As with motivated buyers, if you are respectful and ethical in your dealings with real estate agents and bird dogs, they will want to continue to work with you and bring deals to you.

If you find a property you're interested in, you can send a postcard or a letter to the owners, offering to help solve their problem. If need be, you can find names and addresses in government property tax records.

You may make many, many offers before one is accepted, so patience is incredibly important to finding success in wholesaling. Once you get some momentum behind your business and build your network, you will have more resources for finding good opportunities for investment, but when you dive in you will need the determination to overcome rejection.

KEEP LEARNING!

Now that you know a little bit about investing in real estate, and specifically the strategy of wholesaling, you are in a great position to build on that knowledge. If the financial flexibility and excitement of buying and selling property grabs your interest, you will want to dig much deeper. There are so many resources to seek out, from books to internet forums to seminars to coaches and mentors. Don't cut corners; continue to educate yourself and you'll be in great shape to dive into this exciting field.

KEEP YOUR JOB & GET PROMOTED ...GUARANTEED

Take Control of Your Career In Just 7 Steps

Frantz Forestal

There are a lot of books about the job market —getting a job, losing a job, balancing life and a job, and so on — but there's little to no practical help on keeping your job in a constantly changing world. No one tells you how to take charge of your career and steer it in the direction you want it to go.

Simply said, do you want to be the passenger or the driver in your career?

A passenger goes along doing the job as assigned. He or she assumes that things will go on that way forever. Unfortunately, the world doesn't work that way anymore. You can be in a job for years, only to find that the skills needed have changed, or the job isn't relevant anymore and is being eliminated. Unless you have prepared yourself for a change — seen it coming as it were — you will find yourself out of work, looking for the first job you can get (rather than getting your career back on track).

If you've been a passenger up to now, don't worry. There are things you can do to make sure this never happens to you. More than that: instead of getting fired you can likely get an increase in pay within six months or a year.

A driver, on the other hand, is always watching the road ahead. He or she looks left and right, to see what others in the company are doing, and builds relationships with the right people. A driver also keeps an eye out for changes and trends in the marketplace and learns new skills at every appropriate opportunity.

Putting yourself in the driver's seat may sound difficult, but it doesn't have to be that hard. And it doesn't have to be complicated. There's a straight line to success in any field and, when you create the path to be followed based on the business environment that you're in, you are sure to have created the right road for you. There's no way you're not going to have a good opportunity and be able to grab it.

It doesn't take a Human Relations (HR) manager or a recruiter to show you the way. Achieving your goals is a much more practical matter than most "professional" advice addresses. (Keep in mind, though, that HR people and recruiters can be helpful when you are following your path.) There are proven actions you can take that will put you on the right road and keep you on a straight path to a successful career. Here are the seven steps you need to take to guarantee — and improve — your place in the company.

1. SET UP YOUR FOUNDATION

Learn everything you can about the responsibilities and tasks associated with your job. Get better at them and stay on top of new techniques and tools by taking courses or using self-help books when needed. Be consistent in your strong performance of those responsibilities.

Behave properly while you're working. That means, dress for the next level up, be friendly and helpful (without overdoing it) and act as if you are happy to be there. Position yourself appropriately: If you act like an asset, you will be perceived as an asset.

Become friends with "the right people," both co-workers and managers who can be helpful in your career. Be someone they can trust and count on. Become the go-to person for what you do and explain just enough so that people know they don't know as much as you do about the subject.

2. KNOW WHERE YOUR JOB IS GOING

Another part of doing your job properly is making sure you know where that job is going. Start by asking yourself these questions:

- Is my job fulfilling the needs of today's marketplace?
- If not, what responsibilities or skills would prepare me to serve my clients or customers better?
- Is there an opportunity to create a new position, to meet a need or take advantage of an opportunity that most people don't yet see?
- How might my job change in the near future?
- Will my position even be here in the next five years? Ten years?

- If not, is it time to change careers?

I've benefited from doing this in my own job. I've had great success as a system accountant, something that didn't exist six or seven years ago. No one could have even written the job description in those days, but I saw that there was a problem that needed fixing and made sure that I acquired the necessary skills to fulfill that need as soon as I quickly as I could do so.

Specifically, in those days you were either an IT guy or an accountant. As accounting software became increasingly more important to conducting business, a need arose for someone who could bridge the two positions. (Financial software is mainly about how the database has been built, and how the numbers within it are linked together in different tables or with other databases.) Technical problems were a nightmare because, if you asked an IT person to fix some issues, his or her work might mess up the numbers for the accountant. What was really needed was an accountant who knew the software, so I became one.

3. DON'T PROCRASTINATE, BE PROACTIVE

Once I identified that opportunity, I didn't wait for a potential employer to come looking. I took the initiative, and contacted a recruiter to find out if there were positions available. I also asked about what I would need to do to be ready when a job came up. In other words, I made my interest and intentions known to someone who knew the market better than I did and could be of help to me.

A month or two later, the recruiter called and said that Microsoft® was offering a free class, with certification. The recruiter went on to say that, if I got this certification, he could send me out for a specific position. The software was new, Microsoft was promoting it heavily and, in just a few months, I had a new job. I was a leader in my area, among the first to know and use what has become a standard tool in my market. That made me highly desirable. I was able to negotiate the terms of my employment and even got a signing bonus.

The point of my story is simple. I made my job happen. I knew there was an unfulfilled need, made sure I was aware that there was new software coming and asked the right people for help early on. I dominated the job market because I put myself in the driver's seat.

4. BE A SQUEAKY WHEEL, MAKE YOUR INTENTIONS KNOWN

One of the most important techniques of negotiation is to ask for what you want. No one can read your mind, and bosses don't go around giving out raises or promotions just for the fun of it. Actively pursue the outcome you desire. Make your wishes known and ensure that your manager — and his or her manager — know that you deserve to be rewarded for your accomplishments and achievements. If you've set up a strong foundation, they will understand how valuable you are to the company.

Be realistic in your expectations of how quickly that raise or promotion might occur — these things don't happen overnight — but don't let someone else put you off with promises. Don't accept silence or let your manager ignore you. It may feel like you are being too aggressive but, at some point, if your manager hasn't done anything about your request, you will need to wake him up.

Don't threaten, but make it clear that you are thinking about leaving in the next six months or a year if you don't get what you want. Reiterate your accomplishments and remind him of your value.

5. KNOW YOUR REAL WORTH

You are not just valuable because of what you've already done. There will be financial repercussions if you leave, so you need to know what it will cost the company to replace you. Let's say you make $100,000 a year and decide to leave your job tomorrow. How much money will it take to fill your position?

Well, how long will it take for your manager to replace you? First, there's likely to be a two month process in which he has to request and receive permission from management and HR to fill the position, interview candidates, choose his favorites and have them meet management. Once an offer gets made, there is a period of time for the candidate to accept, give notice and be able to start. It could take four months by the time that new person is up to speed.

So, right away, there is a significant expense to the company if you move on. It could cost up to half your annual salary — in this case, $50,000 — to let you leave. Compare that to the 10% — or even 20% — increase you might be asking for and you can see how compelling a story there is to keeping you happy in your current position.

6. BE PREPARED

At some point, if you haven't received a positive response from those higher up, you will need to consider moving on. Start exploring other job opportunities, ensure that your Curriculum Vitae (CV) is current and pull together a portfolio of your accomplishments. Include any positive emails you've received, relevant certifications, a summary of the projects you've started and other materials that will help build a strong selling message.

You can and should go out for more than one job at a time. Keep looking for better and better opportunities. That's a powerful technique for moving your career ahead. Also, when you meet up with a recruiter, remember that your challenge is not to get the job offered, but to evaluate the opportunity and decide if it is right for you. When you identify a job worth pursuing, remember your worth. Stay in the driver's seat and don't be afraid to negotiate or even say no if the terms are not to your liking.

7. USE YOUR LEVERAGE

Once you have another opportunity, use it to its full advantage. Don't just close the door on your current employer. Dangle your new opportunity in front of your manager like you would a piece of candy in front of a child you want to behave. If you've built a strong foundation and been performing well, it is likely that your manager will not want you to go. He or she will likely think through the situation and talk to HR or higher management about making a counteroffer. If there is a counteroffer, give it serious consideration. Consider the pros and cons of each position and make your decision based on what's best for your long term career.

There's actually one more step you might want to consider.

8. ASK FOR HELP

The seven steps above are proven strategies for taking control of your own career. However, there may be times when you want advice on how to handle a specific situation. Don't be shy about asking for help.

If you are on LinkedIn — and you should be — ask a general question, or look up someone you know who might have experienced a similar situation. Better still, search out website communities like **www.getabigraiseguaranteed.com**, the online resource I founded for just this purpose. You'll be able to read about what others have successfully done within their own companies, or how they determined it was time to move on. Plus, it is a great place to share what's worked for you and a major resource for networking among others in your field.

Evolution of Consciousness for the Entrepreneur

Accelerate Your Consciousness, Master Your Life

Audree Tara Weitzman

"Be the change that you wish to see in the world."

– Mahatma Gandhi

"With great power comes great responsibility"

– Voltaire, Uncle Ben, Spiderman

We have been through the Industrial Evolution, the Scientific Evolution and the Technological Evolution. Now is the time for the Evolution of Consciousness. A term prevalent in the personal growth and transformational communities, the Evolution of Consciousness comes out of the ever growing New Age movement. It involves the process of self-awareness and the awakening of the human mind. In truth, it is about personally understanding and awakening to our own behaviors, belief systems and the answers to two critical questions: "Does this serve me?" and "Do I want to live this way?

What does this have to do with you, the entrepreneur? Self-awareness can be a powerful tool in the development of your success.

YOUR THOUGHTS AND BEHAVIORS CREATE YOUR REALITY

We are facing a critical time in our human history. I say critical because our economy, ecology and the human race are struggling for survival. The stress of maintaining your life and excelling to a better way of living has become unbalanced in the "me" culture that we have become. This struggle for survival has an effect on a personal scale: financial hardships, loss of jobs, market crashes, housing devaluations and a lack of well being. We are living fearful lives and have lost connections to both our inner selves and the outer world around us.

You can say that this cataclysmic way of thinking has gone on for centuries. Why do we now need to become aware of our behaviors and how we live? It is because all that we have accomplished, created and discovered can now be utilized for the self-preservation of the planet and the human race. We can take what we have learned and create a way of life that supports community, growth, prosperity and the regeneration of a damaged ecology. I see the Evolution of Consciousness as a coming together of all the past evolutionary processes, and the using of our higher awareness to shift and change the way we live in the world. We can then create a world where we are living to our fullest potential.

So, how does an entrepreneur fit into this world of instability and chaos? Every entrepreneur is a visionary. You think outside the box. Your thoughts and belief systems control who you are and what you become. You are looking for a way to succeed beyond what is expected of you. At the same time, however, everyone else in your life has his or her limited thoughts and belief systems. The outside support for your great adventure (owning your own business) is, therefore, weak, or sometimes non-existent. The evolution of your consciousness and the awareness of your mind's thoughts and belief systems will be your strongest supporter on the road to success.

Human beings are automatically hardwired for failure. It is ingrained in our being that we are less than perfect. Most people live their lives with minds full of negative thoughts. Those thoughts keep telling them they are not good enough, or that they do not have the power to create an amazing life. In fact, those thoughts often say "you do not deserve to have an amazing life". On average, people walk through life sick, poor and lacking enthusiasm or joy for life. They go to school, and then work at a job that meets less than their fullest potential.

You are the exception. For you, there is one big difference in life; you have a dream to do something different. You want to make a difference or do something better than anyone else does. How are you going to accomplish your dreams and live to your fullest potential with all the obstacles knocking at your door? The secret is to evolve your consciousness.

Consciousness by definition means to be aware or have self-awareness. To evolve your consciousness is to follow a process that leads to an unfolding of your self-awareness — that is, the awareness of how you live and behave according to your thoughts and belief systems. And, the evolved consciousness of an entrepreneur is a mindset that allows you to transform yourself continuously into the most successful you. You can then live your life purpose, be in a state of well being and accomplish your heart's desire.

Imagine what it will be like when you are acting and living in your highest potential. Your business, branding, marketing, the operations of your company and your relationships —with yourself, your partners and employees, your audience and clients — will all flow in an effortless way. Imagine your life flowing in abundance, with the ability to see your visions clearly and to manifest your dreams into reality. That is what the evolution of your consciousness will do for you. That is why your Evolution of Consciousness is the most important piece of the puzzle, your greatest tool for success.

THE PROCESS OF AN EVOLVED CONSCIOUSNESS

So how do you become this evolved conscious mastermind of business and personal success? How do you evolve into your fullest potential? There is a guided process to give you the tools you need to clear out the old patterning and create an awakening. The steps are:

1. Acquiring the knowledge or belief that everything is energy.

The first step involves understanding and adopting the belief that you are made up of energy. Actually, everything is energy — a vibrational frequency of wave-like patterns that make up our universe. Energy is an electromagnetic charge that is within and surrounds your body Material objects are slow moving vibrational frequencies (energy) that make up matter. Thoughts are fast moving vibrational frequencies that are invisible to the naked eye, but still move and create our reality. This concept is sometimes abstract, but there is a lot of information to research at your leisure. You may want to read about The Law of Attraction or about manifesting your visions into reality. You might also watch the movie "The Secret".

As an entrepreneur, your greatest tool will be your knowledge of energy and how to manage it to master your life, your relationships and your business. Energy affects how we are in relationship to ourselves and others. It impacts how we feel on a daily basis and how our vision of life's purpose or our business is projected and manifested into the world.

For example, there are some people who, for no reason, you just cannot seem to like. They are very negative, and you feel drained when you see them. Then, there are other people who you love to be around because they are happy, have a glow about them and are especially positive. You might say it's about how they act or behave, but it is really about the energy that they put out into the world. The same goes for your business. If you know about energy you can shift the energies in your life to attract the clients you want.

Importantly, your energy moves based on your thought process. That is why they say if you have negative thoughts you will get sick. This is true. Your thoughts create energy. In an instant, you can shift your negative thoughts to positive ones. And in turn you can change your negative energy into positive energy. In sum, *"Energy goes where consciousness flows"*.

Energy is an inherent tool at your disposal; a tool that, if you choose not to use, will be there anyway, reacting to your subconscious mind, an event, which you do not want to happen in your life.

2. Grounding your energy so that you become a stable force of energy.

Life is chaos. Constantly shifting, moving and changing. There is no way to predict or control what happens in your life. This is the cause of all stress, anxiety and grief. I see life, especially during times of transformation, as a tornado swirling around you. It becomes very difficult to deal with things or to make the proper decisions (or even function, for that matter) when life is coming at you like a storm. The drama of life picks you up and lands you in any place, usually on the top of your head. And, for an entrepreneur, this tornado takes on speed and velocity, tenfold. Flying by the seat of your pants is an understatement.

If you are not careful, the decision-making process can mean life or death for your business, your dreams, your life purpose and your financial stability. Grounding your energy will allow you to be calm and stable while the chaos of life is swirling about you. You can become the calm in the center of the storm. In this calm place, you are able to see the whole picture of what is in front of you, and you will no longer be held hostage by emotional reactions to any drama. There is a centered feeling within you, and that is when you will be most effective.

In my training as a healer, I have found that grounding meditation is the foundation for any energy/healing work. You cannot be effective at moving energy if you are not grounded. You cannot make important life altering or business altering decisions if you are not grounded.

To make stable calm decisions, your energy needs to be in your body. I know that sounds a bit strange but, as humans, we have the habit of moving our energies up and outside of our physical bodies. We are not even aware of what we are doing. The energy leaves the physical body because of the emotional pain and suffering that we experience from life; it is easier to cope when we do not feel the pain.

When the energetic body is not connected to the physical form, it causes the body to feel anxious. It can cause a sense of being out of control, unsafe. This experience may cause physical symptoms like heart palpitations and other unproductive side effects. Think about a balloon on a string that is not connected to anything else. The balloon floats away. That is your energy and your consciousness floating away and, with it, the ability to function effectively.

Actually, it is extremely important to ground your energy into the earth itself. Some people have done yoga or used other techniques, such as guided meditation, and imagined roots growing from their feet into the ground. These techniques are based on centuries old teachings that say to anchor your body energy into the earth about three to four feet. There is real science behind these practices. There are electromagnetic grids in the earth's surface, and we connect the energy body into the earth's electromagnetic grids. This gives us a sense of security, belonging and calm.

In 2004, while doing my grounding techniques for meditation and healing work, I discovered a relatively new technique. I was forced to go deeper into the earth to ground my energy. I felt the connection of my energy field anchoring into something very powerful. What I have since learned is that I was anchoring into a permanent electromagnetic field of the earth. Although there is no science as of yet to validate what I was doing, through time and experience I have found this to be a very powerful grounding technique. I have taught it to many of my clients, some with stage four cancers, some facing terminal illnesses (they are in various places of instability).

I also have used this technique with my clients going through life transitions and major upheavals, as well as with those needing to feel safe and calm before making important life decisions. My clients who have used this grounding technique instantaneously felt an improved state of being. There is no waiting; the improved state of being happens as soon as you do the technique.

And, with practice, this technique becomes so easy that it is requires just a quick thought to become grounded; your consciousness and your physical body are calm, centered and balanced in a way that makes you feel safe and unaffected by what is happening around you. You will then begin to live and function through non-emotional reactions to the chaos and drama of life. This will be a great tool in your daily functioning. And, it can determine your success rate in making important business and life decisions.

To learn about this technique and how to use it on your own, please visit (**evolve2b.com…password: onlyone**).

3. Using energy to clear your negative thoughts and belief systems.

The entrepreneur is a master visionary. The spark of his or her thoughts and the dreams that they build, lead to the creation of a product or business, to fill the needs of the many. Entrepreneurs go against society's grain and the protests of the subconscious mind. Then there is the ego; everyone is watching you, secretly wanting you to fail. Or your own self-sabotage tries to take you down — not to mention how nerve-wracking it can be to make all the correct decisions about branding and marketing yourself and your business.

As an entrepreneur, your mindset must be clear and clean of any negative thoughts. Since thoughts are energy, they can literally reach out and affect your relationship with the outside world. It is, therefore, imperative that you erase any negative thoughts from your mind. Being successful is based on how well you manage and clear your thoughts, your consciousness and your energy.

So, what are negative thoughts? They are the ones that speak to you in your mind and judge everything that you do. Sometimes they are things your parents have told you, or they are based on experiences you had in the past. Some thoughts are from you, telling yourself you are not worthy, good enough, smart enough, do not have any money; the list goes on.

Then there are thoughts of your own greatness, how amazing you are and how no one can beat you or your product. Those thoughts will get you in trouble too; in business a thought can keep you from paying attention to improving your products or services.

In sum, thoughts are your ego, and your ego is a manifestation of an untruth. It is how you perceive yourself and the world based on past experiences. The ego makes up stories for us to believe and cuts us off from having an experience based in the present moment. It is the ego that will destroy your hopes and dreams. This is not ego bashing; the ego has long served you and has been a great asset in so many ways. But it has been running the "show" for your whole life. Now, to reach your fullest potential and the best life or business you can create, your ego needs to take a step back. At **evolve2b.com,** I give you a tool to clear your negative mind set gracefully, quickly and easily.

The process of the Evolution of Consciousness is the empowerment of you taking responsibility for your life. You become the master of your reality and create the life or business that you desire. When you are aware of your negative thoughts and behavior patterns, and you make the decision to let them go, you move into a place of positive thoughts, and begin to manifest a very powerful reality for yourself. This reality is filled with a presence of your own truth, living in the moment and knowing that you have the ability and tools to have what you desire.

4. Manifesting your desires from the heart.

The concept of manifesting your desires (or creating your reality) is something that has been much talked about in the past few years. When the movie, "The Secret," came out, it introduced the idea that it is possible to have the life you desire by asking for it. In fact, "The Secret" became the most popular source of information on manifesting and The Law of Attraction. What the movie doesn't mention is that this information about manifesting your desire, is based in an old paradigm (knowledge) used in a time when the earth vibrated at a different energetic frequency. There is a science to it, which you can read about in detail in my book, *Body Of Light, the Evolution of Consciousness Through the New Chakra System*.

The crucial point coming out of that science is that something about The Law of Attraction has changed and, so, the technique for manifesting has changed. Now, energy is very fast moving, and that changes the way we relate to ourselves and each other. We are coming into the world of peace; we are shifting into an era of living in our hearts. Why is that important for manifestation?

The old way to manifest was to have a vision which would shift your thoughts and move the energy to create your desires. Easy, right? It works, but is problematic in that, often, along with the thought of what you wanted, came a thought of how it might be impossible or that you are unworthy, In that case, the negative thought canceled out the vision.

The solution in this new energy is not to have a vision. Instead, go deeper, out of your mind (where the vision is) and into your heart, where your desire is. Yes, the heart is where manifestation takes place in this new era! For a great tool to teach you how to manifest from the heart and experience manifestation in this higher vibrational energy, please go to **(evolve2b.com)**.

To create and manifest what you desire into reality, it must be done from the heart. There can be no attachment to how it manifests. There is no business plan for manifestation. That is not The Law of Attraction. The Law of Attraction says like energies (thoughts move energy) attract to each other and what you desire will manifest. The most powerful energetic wave patterns are in the heart.

... the heart is far more than a simple pump ... (it is) a highly complex, self-organized information processing center with its own functional "brain" that communicates with and influences the cranial brain... These influences profoundly affect brain function and most of the body's major organs, and ultimately determine the quality of life." — **The Institute of HeartMath**

If you are going into business to create destruction or greed, the techniques I've been talking about are not for you; it won't work. Those negative emotions are low vibrational frequencies and thought forms and will no longer be tolerated in this new paradigm. However, If you are envisioning a business product or service to help make the world a better place because you know that you can improve on a system, or want to make a difference in the world and in your life, then this knowledge will work. These tools can only be used for the highest good of man.

Remember that the mind is not a perfected state of being where there are no negative thoughts. You must drop all of your vision into your heart. Breathe in your business plan — not the step-by-step process, but the end result of your goals and vision. Feel what it is like to have your successful business, all the support that you need and beyond what you can imagine. Expect that you will have the life of your dreams, feel what it's like to live in that place of complete happiness and then let it go. When negative thoughts come into your mind, use the tools I gave you to release them.

5. Stepping into the new paradigm of business and living your highest potential.

Once you have learned this process of understanding and harnessing your body energies for good, you will be able to create and manifest the business of your dreams — no, more than that — a business beyond your wildest dreams. This is especially true for entrepreneurs because coming from an evolved consciousness means that you will:

- Maintain calm and balance to make important decisions
- Clear your limiting negative thoughts and belief systems
- Living your fullest potential, vibrant and healthy — physically mentally emotional and spiritually
- Be able to manifest your desires quickly and easily

Nothing in your business, or your life, will ever be the same.

Audree Weitzman uses her knowledge and skill as a healer, reads the Akashic Records and incorporates her training in energy based life coaching into a formula she developed called Intuitive Strategies Coaching, please go to evolve2b.com for more information

Declutter Your Mind for Success

Erin Muldoon Stetson

"**M**y baggage", "your baggage", "his baggage" —phrases thrown around in casual conversation as much as an actual suitcase is thrown around by handlers at an airport. What does it mean when we talk about our "baggage?" After all, we're not actually referring to that matching set of luggage your mother bought you after college, are we? No, we are talking about the emotional and life experience "stuff" you pick up along the way; the stuff that weighs you down and makes the inside of your head hurt.

When we take a trip, our baggage literally gets heavier and messier with each souvenir we add. And, if you're like me, you can't wait to unpack and put the dirty laundry in the wash where it belongs. Similarly, in life every experience comes with emotional as well as physical stuff. Unfortunately, not all of it is as pleasurable as the mementos from vacation. Plus, when unpacking, most of us take a look at what comes out of the suitcase so we can put it where it belongs.

But, when it comes to emotional baggage, people tend to stuff it away without really looking at it. What they are doing is filling up the emotional equivalent of a classic, overstuffed closet; the one where, when you open the door, a thousand things come crashing down on your head. The one where you don't open the door except maybe a couple inches now and then to stuff more things into the dark, scary closet.

On an emotional level, that stuffing is doing you no good at all. In fact, all that clutter is not relegated to your subconscious mind. It affects all parts of your mind, as well as your body and spirit. It causes pain, disease and emotional issues. It can block you in countless ways—from achieving your potential, living authentically and manifesting abundance in your life.

Why is your mind so cluttered in the first place? It's because you've been "collecting" experiences, memories and feelings for a lifetime. Even in the womb, there may have been alarming and confusing experiences. If you had a difficult birth, or traumatic first few moments of life, the imprint of those experiences is still with you. To add insult to injury, as a baby, you may have often struggled to be understood or to have your needs met while your bumbling care givers tried to figure out if you were hungry, sleepy or needed a diaper change. How frustrating that must have been. Those early experiences went into your collection.

Think about the clutter you have collected. I suggest that, as you read this, you jot down the thoughts that pop into your head. No doubt you will start to think of your own personal clutter that is stuffed inside you somewhere. Your notes will help you when you decide to clear that clutter out. Remember, you need to look at all of it squarely before you can put it away for good.

The collection of emotional clutter goes on throughout your life. In the toddler years, you stumble and fall (literally), and struggle to communicate only to be utterly misunderstood. Then, as a teen, you stumble figuratively as you try to find your way, and still find communication difficult as your values change in relation to those of parents, teachers or even your peers.

Think about it:

- A humiliating experience in class when a teacher scolded you in front of everyone.
- Someone you had a crush on treated you with contempt.
- A vicious, behind-the-back bullying campaign waged by an alleged "friend."
- A time when you were unkind or ungrateful to someone who didn't deserve it.
- The day you walked out of a store with a pack of gum you didn't pay for.

Each of these experiences is jarring. Every single one of them can disrupt the energy system in your body and mind. It's no wonder you feel so overwhelmed with the clutter.

I vividly remember something that happened when I was 12 years old. I received a scathing note from one of my "best friends" who happened to live across the street. It was poetic in its poignancy. "Erin, you think you're hot shit on a silver platter, but really you're just cold diarrhea on a paper plate!" Wow. That hurt. It's funny now —I mean really funny — and I'm so impressed with the verbiage. But at the time, I cried big tears —the kind of tears that I thought might never stop gushing. I had to re-think my whole persona. Did I really think that I was "hot shit?" And was I actually "just cold diarrhea?" I collected the anger, the sadness and the insecurity of that moment and buried it all in my mind, heart and body.

For the record, I'm not saying that any of the experiences I'm mentioning were bad, or good, for that matter. Nor am I saying that my friend in the "hot shit" story was wrong for writing that note. What I am saying is that our experiences stay with us, in one form or another, and often create disruptions in our energy systems.

Have you been able to jot down a few notes about memories of your own that may have stayed with you and created disruptions in your own life? Job struggles, relationship or parenting challenges, heartache, loss, trauma—the little things and the big things that may be stuffed away, buried, doing some damage unbeknownst to you.

All of these things go into your collection. Don't judge them. Don't judge yourself. Simply write down a "title" for the memory. We'll address it later and possibly let go of it with ease. You won't lose the memory, but merely the negative charge that is connected to it.

Now that you have started to examine your impressive collection, you can understand how it has grown exponentially over your lifetime. You can imagine how your mind has gotten cluttered. It's no wonder so many people feel weighed down, bottled up, distracted and even confused at times.

It is possible to declutter your mind if you have the proper tools. There is a process you can use to fix the effects of that build-up.

Pat yourself on the back for beginning this journey. It's going to be fun!

TAPPING

Tapping is based on Emotional Freedom Techniques (EFT). It is a relatively new discovery that has provided thousands with relief from pain, disease and emotional issues. It can alleviate the most common matters (fear of public speaking) to the most extreme (chronic debilitating back pain), and a wide array of "stuff" in between. Basically, tapping is mind/body healing. It is a combination of ancient Chinese knowledge and modern psychology.

Tapping produces a relaxation response in your body and mind and creates an emotional contentment in the present moment. It is wonderfully simple and effective, and it is accomplished by stimulating well established energy meridian points on your body.

"How do you do that?"

You do that by tapping on particular points with your fingertips while focusing on the issue at hand. "

Really?" "It's not more complicated than that?"

Yes, really. And no, it's not more complicated than that. Plus, the process is easy to memorize, and portable—you can do it anywhere. You only need your hands and your mind.

It is my goal to make this real healing easy and accessible to you. For the entrepreneur feeling overwhelmed, or the person who has dreams of starting a business but is blocked by fear, these techniques can help create such fundamental shifts that walls tumble and doors open. The healing path of body, mind and spirit lies ahead.

So how does tapping differ, say, from other energy healing modalities such as acupuncture? By focusing on the mind-body connection, EFT tapping harnesses the power of the mind and combines it with the body's energy to propel healing to a level that could not otherwise be achieved. The techniques essentially bring a psychotherapeutic element to the energy meridians long familiar to alternative healers.

The power of thought and its effects on our well-being are no longer considered theoretical. The evidence is piling up. So let's declutter your mind so that your thoughts no longer sabotage you but can have the impact you want them to!

EFT TAPPING IN ACTION

Let's look at a particular, very real scenario that will be familiar to many. I like to call it the fear of public writing. Now, we could also address the fear of public speaking or something else but, given the fact that I overcame my fear of public writing to write this chapter, it seems an apropos example. Additionally, the fear of public writing can be a huge deal for an entrepreneur, especially when you are expected to publish a blog, post on Facebook and update your website on a regular basis.

EFT tapping has the unique ability to handle your fears and turn them into calm cool action. Whether you feel paralyzed at the thought of doing an activity like writing, or are shy about sharing what you've already written, EFT tapping can help put those fears in check.

For example, have you hesitated to write a book because of your anxiety about the fact that the dreaded written word can never be erased? It will be "out there" speaking for you, for all time. If you are like I was, that thought paralyzes you. But here I am, writing this. And enjoying it, I might add. How am I able to face my fears so courageously?

As I mentioned above, the answer is quite simple and incredibly revolutionary. I can't wait to share this fabulous secret with you. Tap along with me. You won't be sorry. Then we can high five on the other side of this silly fear that's holding you back from your greatness.

EFT IN A NUTSHELL

The body contains a network of energy points and energy channels — actual locations that can be accessed through tapping. In addition to the physical act of tapping on these specific points, EFT involves the use of words. The power of words, of language, to channel and manifest intention is hardly in question any more. So with EFT, you will use words first to acknowledge the details of the negative — the big pieces of junk cluttering your mind.

Looking at them and facing them is the first step to releasing the junk you've been shoving into your suitcase for so long. Finally, positive language is used to manifest what you want to bring into your life after you've "put away" the clutter where it belongs. Where is that? It's where your clutter can no longer hurt you.

So, let's return to our hypothetical case of a person (maybe you) who is afraid to write. This fear is getting in the way of your business, your success and your ability to create abundance in your life. Below are the simple steps that I would walk you through if you were this hypothetical person. In no time, you would be writing and publishing.

STEP 1

Close your eyes and think about what is holding you back from writing and publishing that book or updating your blog. Once you have something specific in mind, give it a number on a scale of 0-10, ten being the most intense. If you have many things running through your mind, write them down and start with the one specific issue that has the highest intensity. Think of it as the biggest piece of junk in that closet—the one that might actually knock you out if it fell on your head. Give that piece of junk a "title"—you don't need to write down the whole sordid history or explanation of the issue, just its title. The number you assign to that issue is extremely important. It allows you to compare how you feel before and after tapping.

For example, you may be thinking: "What if my ex reads this and thinks, 'what the %&*# is she writing about? Why was I ever with that chick? What a weirdo!'" Or perhaps you are thinking, "No one who reads this will ever want to talk to me, meet me or hire me. I'll be ruined."

Your title for this piece of mental debris might be: Fear of Rejection. Maybe it earns a level of 8, 9 or even 10, depending on how paralyzing it is. (You insert whichever number makes sense for how you feel in the present moment.)

STEP 2

Tap continuously with your fingers on each of the following spots while repeating the corresponding phrases out loud. (If you think a diagram might be helpful, please visit http://taponit.com.)

Karate Chop Spot (this is the place on the side of your hand you would use if you were to use a karate chop to break a piece of wood): Tap continuously with four fingers on that spot while saying the following phrase three times aloud: "Even though I am afraid of being judged and rejected [insert here: by my ex or by future clients] for what I write, I'm still a really good person."

- **Eyebrow point** (this is the beginning of your eyebrow closest to your nose): Tap continuously with two fingers at that spot and repeat the following phrase: "I'm afraid that my [ex or future client] is going to judge me and my writing in a negative way." Repeat Once.

- **Side of eye** (this is the bone bordering the outside corner of your eye): Tap continuously with two fingers on that spot and repeat the following phrase: "What if my [ex or future client] reads what I wrote and thinks I'm a terrible writer?" Repeat Once.

- **Under the eye** (about ½ inch below): Tap continuously with two fingers, saying: "I'm nervous to put myself out there. I will be laughed at." Repeat once.

- **Under the nose** (this is the philtrum: the small indentation between the bottom of your nose and the top of your upper lip): Tap continuously with two fingers on that spot while you say: "I'm afraid that someone [my ex or a judgmental future client] is going to read my writing if I put it out there." Repeat once.

- **Chin** (the spot midway between the bottom of your chin and your lower lip): Tap continuously with two fingers on that spot and say: "I'm not sure if I can handle the embarrassment of having my writing judged by [my ex, a future client] or anyone else for that matter." Repeat once.

- **Collarbone**: Tap continuously with four fingers along your collarbone towards your breast bone. Say these words: "I'm not ready to have my thoughts and ideas critiqued and ridiculed." Repeat once.

- **Under arm** (four inches below your armpit, on the side of your body): Tap continuously with four fingers: "I'm nervous that [my ex or a future client] will read what I'm writing and make fun of me." Repeat once.

- **Crown of head**: Tap continuously with all five fingers in a circular motion on the top of your head: "I'm afraid that [my ex or anyone] is going to read my writing and laugh at me." Repeat once.

- **Eyebrow point**: "I'm okay now." Repeat once.

- **Side of eye**: "I can relax now." Repeat once.

- **Under the eye**: "I am calm and relaxed." Repeat once.

- **Under the nose**: "My confidence is growing." Repeat once.

- **Chin**: "I am feeling more and more confident about my writing." Repeat once.

- **Collarbone**: "I am excited to write an awesome [book, article, blog]." Repeat once.

- **Under arm**: "I can't wait to write my [book, article, blog]." Repeat once.

- **Top of head**: "I'm ready to write and publish an amazing [book, article, blog]." Repeat once.

When you are done, take a deep breath and hold it. Then let it out in a slow, smooth exhalation.

STEP 3

After completing the tapping and repetitions, reassess the intensity of your feelings about the topic (in this case, public writing), using the scale you used originally, from 0 to 10, with ten being the strongest. Write down your response, the number and something about how you feel. Comment about whether there were any qualitative changes to the way you view or feel about the topic. If your number is still high, then repeat the process.

Be clear in acknowledging any change. For example, "After tapping, my fear of rejection and judgment regarding my writing from [my ex or future clients] is at about a level two, down significantly from my previous level of eight."

The three steps outlined above are how you use EFT to overcome your fear of public writing. You can use the same format to cope with other issues that are holding you back. The phrases that you use in your repetitions during tapping will vary according to what you are trying to release. Here are some examples:

- **Karate Chop Spot**: "Even though I'm afraid that my family will disown me because what I want to write about is too off the grid for them, I have confidence and love. I forgive them for their potential judgments." Repeat three times.

- **Karate Chop Spot**: "Even though I fear that my ideas will change one day, and what I write will be 'out there' forever, reminding me of how foolish I was, I deeply and completely love and accept myself."

- **Karate Chop Spot**: "Even though my writing isn't perfect, it's a work in progress that never seems to end. I am whole, and complete, and fabulous just as I am right now, and so is my writing."

- **Karate Chop Spot**: "Even though I feel as if I don't have time to write, I am willing to make changes in my life because I deeply and completely love and accept myself."

The intended and very real outcome of EFT tapping in this circumstance is increased self-confidence. Whether it is your writing or something else that is standing in your way, your confidence will grow exponentially the more you tap. You will laugh at your previous fears. To use our example of fearing the reaction of your ex, once you have utilized EFT tapping, you might assume that, should he read your writing, he'll wonder how he ever let someone like you get away!

Our fears about what might happen are often times more intense than any actual, potential outcome. Tapping creates equilibrium between that fear and what is real. It will allow you to gain a calm, cool perspective regarding the debris that was weighing you down by cluttering up your suitcase or your closet –in other words, your mind!

Decluttering your mind through EFT tapping applies to literally any aspect of your life. It can help you find fulfillment, success, and enjoyment in any arena: relationships, money, body image, health etc. Starting with identifying what is holding you back, seeing it for what it is and then releasing it, you ultimately replace it with something wholesome that will help you move forward.

The things that are holding you back are all that junk we talked about earlier: Fears or objections (the "I can't" mentality), obstacles — perceived or real (time, logistics) — and ultimately your "story" – the belief system that holds you where you are instead of helping you get to where you want to be.

The process that works for your mind can also be used to declutter your body. There is a holistic connection between and among mind, body and spirit, which means that detoxing one will help you declutter the others.

Your spirit can be decluttered and detoxified too. In using EFT techniques for the spirit, you will address matters of perspective, outlook and attitude.

The law of attraction is essentially at work every time you succumb to fear or, conversely, feel optimistic. When you fear an outcome and fixate on that fear, you are focusing on what is essentially a belief system based on fear. Your mind, as well as your actions, reflects that belief system and you will manifest the very things you are afraid of.

When you can tap on and release the fear, you can recreate a belief system based on positive emotions, optimism and confidence. You become that person and your every action reflects those new beliefs.

So what does this mean for you? It means that EFT tapping can bring you more comfort, love and enjoyment in life. It can help you rid yourself of the heavy baggage and clutter that get in the way of being your most successful self.

To learn more about the benefits of tapping, please visit http://taponit.com.

The Print Management Specialist

How to Get the Best Job for the Best Price with the Least Stress

Thomas J. Samuelson

Imagine that you are an entrepreneur who wants to manufacture an energy drink. You have a great recipe, and you want to get your delicious and invigorating drink on store shelves and into the hands of teenagers, athletes and coaches across the country as quickly as possible.

Maybe you have lined up a factory that will manufacture your beverage. Maybe you have your "brand," but what about packaging and sales materials?

Your business is small. You don't have a lot of dedicated staff who can design your graphics, find a printer for your labels or find a bottle manufacturer. And then, you find out that most bottle companies don't make lids. Who's going to make the lids? You need some kind of shipping box, too, or maybe some snazzy inserts. Will that be done by a different printer than the one who took care of the labels? And, of course, schedule and budget are issues. Can you afford the time to make a thousand phone calls, trying to find competitive pricing on all that has to be done?

Plus, how will you coordinate it all? Who will get the bottles, lids and labels to the bottler? Who will put the labels on the bottles and place the bottles into the boxes? It's so complex. You wonder: "How does this work, how much will it cost, how long will it take and who will look out for the integrity of my brand? And, most importantly, will I be happy with the outcome?"

CAN ANYONE OUT THERE TAKE CARE OF ALL THAT PRINTING AND PACKAGING?

Much of what needs to happen has to do with two things: printing and coordinating all the pieces of the specific project. Many businesses these days try to keep overhead down by not hiring in-house staff to keep track of the pieces of this jigsaw puzzle. If you do not personally have the expertise, time and money to define the specifications for each part of the job, to select manufacturers for each aspect of the job, and to manage the projects once they are underway, what will you do? Naturally you don't want to shortchange your job at any stage along the way, but it can be pretty overwhelming.

IS THERE A WAY TO STAY WITHIN BUDGET AND TIME FRAME?

You need a print management specialist. What is that, you may ask? Well, first, let's back up. Once upon a time, businesses like yours had relationships with local printers. When those companies needed shipping labels, business cards, brochures or display materials, they went to their printer to see what he or she could do for them.

There were limitations to this process. If the print shop was a small operation, part of your job was probably outsourced at some expense. Your printer was busy, and could not actually shop around, but had a relationship with someone reliable who could print the bigger pieces that his machines couldn't handle (to use a typical example). This outsourced part of the job would be done at a premium. Why? No competition. Your printer would call and say, "Can you do this?" His contact would answer, "Sure. Here's what it will cost."

A better option is to work with a middle-man who works for a large printing firm — a sales representative for that company. The rep's job is to work with you on your whole project, putting the pieces together. However, you must be aware that the rep is committed to one manufacturer – his or her employer. That, of course, affects his recommendations.

Printing has become such a diverse, varied industry that the old ways are quickly fading. Figuring out what you need, who can do it and how to keep costs down has become a huge job. It takes a long time to scour the field for all the pieces to the puzzle. Not only that, but most suppliers in this field do not deal with the public anymore. Nowadays, many printers keep overhead low by not hiring sales reps and not keeping a storefront. Instead, they do business with the client through an independent middle-man — a print broker.

Print brokers specialize in coordinating your print jobs. Like a conductor, who does not actually play an instrument in the symphony, the print broker does not actually have printing equipment; he pulls the pieces of a job together. The broker does not work for the print providers; he or she works for you, the client. You are his responsibility. The printers, in fact, must work hard to remain competitive as they bid for jobs, thus bringing your costs down.

A good independent broker acts as a free agent, negotiating with any number of printers to get you the best deal on the whole job. All the research, legwork, number crunching and negotiating are done by the broker. However, the print broker's expertise is limited by their experience. They generally concentrate their efforts in basic areas of printing, and may not be able to handle all of your needs.

So let's sum up. We have printers, typically local operations who have limited services and only certain equipment. They do most of the job according to their capabilities (not necessarily your desires), and often outsource the parts they can't do at a premium.

Then we have reps and brokers. Reps will negotiate with you to sell you a job on behalf of their employer, a large printing concern. The work might be good, but the costs may not. Plus, a rep will often tell a small business owner that something can't be done simply because the company he works for can't do it.

A broker, on the other hand, will negotiate with printers to get them to bid competitively, will find printers with the right capabilities for each part of your project and will oversee the details for you. A broker sounds like a good idea, right? But in the end, he's not a full service printer. He's simply a middle-man. A broker has your budget and needs covered, but his ability to fulfill all of the printing and packaging needs may be limited.

MEET TOM THE PRINT MANAGEMENT SPECIALIST

Contrast the previous options with a print management specialist, who is both a printer *and* a broker. He or she is the wave of the future, capable of seeing you through the complexities of all your printing and packaging needs.

The print management specialist has connections with a variety of designers, graphic artists, printers and manufacturers to take care of all of your projects. The entire job can be taken care of, from soup to nuts, without any strain and stress on your part. And, it will be taken care of *by an expert.*

Here's how it works—one-stop shopping at its very best. The print management specialist will create value for you, manage the schedule and correctly coordinate with you from the beginning idea to the final product — all while maintaining the integrity of your brand. The print management specialist is doubly invested in the job. He not only orchestrates the project, his personal reputation as a professional and a specialist is on the line as well.

Let me give you an example. I remember one job in particular that involved everything from getting DVDs replicated, to packaging them in labeled jewel cases, to boxing and shipping the finished product. My extensive list of contacts allowed me to find the best price for my customer in terms of the replication of the DVDs and acquisition of the jewel cases, printing the inserts, making the boxes, then packaging, boxing and shipping the product.

What that meant for my client was that all she had to do was deliver the original recording to me. We went over her wishes regarding graphics and how to incorporate her logo, and I took care of the rest, coordinating with the four suppliers I had lined up, ensuring that each part of the job was done on time. She did not have the time or staff to coordinate all of that on her own, nor could she have done it for the same price, since she would have been dealing with retailers rather than wholesalers. The job was done on schedule and within her budget.

A print management specialist has another distinct advantage over a run-of-the-mill broker — printing experience. As an example, I have forty years of experience working in, managing, and owning print shops. Someone with my experience knows exactly how to help a potential customer envision a project while keeping an eye on the budget.

Let me explain. Let's say you have a big project. You are going to be presenting at a trade show, and need everything from brochures and folders to display materials. You have a vision of how you want things to look. For part of the job you would like foil overlay, for a shiny, high quality image. If you take this job to a regular print shop, you might simply be told that this job cannot be done within your budget constraints.

Here's where working with a print management specialist could make all the difference. What a specialist understands is that there are options. For example, he or she may tell you that you can get a similar effect less expensively by printing on foil paper and using UV ink. If the print shop you are working with does not have that capability or experience, you will never find out about that option. You will have to settle for a final product that does not measure up to your original vision.

This situation can take any form. A print management specialist will know what companies are the best and most cost-competitive to produce not only the printing, but the dye-cutting, the UV coating, the embossing or whatever the customer wants. The customer knows, "I need boxes." A printer says, "Okay, I can do boxes." Meanwhile, the customer never finds out about the other options, if that particular printer hasn't the capability to offer any. Is it going to be a corrugated box? And E-flute box? A collapsible plastic box? An auto-bottom box? Should it have a cut-out foam insert to protect the product?

The industry today encompasses so many possibilities, so many processes and so many products that a single printer is at a distinct disadvantage. A print management specialist has the expertise to offer the customer a myriad of possibilities. For one thing, he is already in the business. In addition, he knows the entire industry and is worth his weight in gold if he has a huge contact list. Experience and longevity are the factors here.

Going back to our original scenario—your energy drink. Let's look at that job through the eyes of an experienced print management specialist. The print manager has the experience, the staff and the connections to acquire the bottles, caps and sleeves; print the labels, boxes and inserts; produce the bottling and packaging, and can even broker the filling of the bottles.

You, the small business owner, no longer have the stress of overseeing the process. You do not have to find competitive providers or manufacturers, no longer have to answer countless emails and phone calls along the way—the print management specialist will raise the level of professionalism by handling all of the above. He will also oversee the budget and the timing and, working with his specialized associates, view how all the printed materials work together to present a unified image consistent with your brand. Each step of the project is approved by you as the project progresses. The integrity of your product is guaranteed, with no worries about your blood pressure!

WHAT IF THERE IS NO PRINT MANAGEMENT SPECIALIST IN YOUR AREA?

Your location and that of your print management specialist don't matter so much. In this day of advanced technology and seemingly space-age internet capabilities, not to mention efficient and fast transportation options, proximity is not particularly vital. You and your print management specialist can converse on the phone, send material and information back and forth via email, and approve graphics and cost-analyses through email as well (or even overnight messenger).

What does have more pertinence is your print manager's proximity to the manufacturing facilities on his contact list. Having the ability to examine the process and product in person will allow your manager to meet your needs fully. Proximity between the manager of the project and the outsourced providers can also shave off time. That can be all-important when adherence to a schedule is vital to your professionalism, as well as that of your print management specialist.

To recap, here are the essentials that should underlie your decision making process when you are looking to get your product designed, printed, packaged, labeled and shipped.

- It is not unusual for a complex print and packaging project to run through four or more manufacturers and providers before it is completed.

- With a print management specialist, all of that work can be done for the most competitive price available. The project is coordinated in such a way as to generate the most efficient outcome of what is a rather fragmented process.

- A good print management specialist has the expertise and wherewithal to plan for the whole course of the job.

- Handling and coordinating transitions with precision is invaluable to your bottom line and your schedule. Having a print management specialist integrate your entire process (remember the energy drink story we started with) prevents waste and delay, both of which can be costly.

- Working with a print management specialist means taking advantage of the specialist's experience as both as a printer and a broker—the best of both worlds.

WHERE CAN I GO FOR MORE PACKAGING AND PRINTING SOLUTIONS?

For more information on packaging and printing projects please visit my website **www.MrPrintUSA.com**. To discuss your future products and receive a free consultation, feel free to contact me at **tom@mrprintusa.com**. Who knows? Ask for a quality cost comparison on your current project and you may be surprised!

www.ingramcontent.com/pod-product-compliance
Lightning Source LLC
Chambersburg PA
CBHW071850230426
43671CB00012B/2132